Nut Butter Universe

Also by Robin Robertson

Fresh from the Vegan Slow Cooker

Quick-Fix Vegan

1,000 Vegan Recipes

Vegan on the Cheap

Vegan Fire & Spice

Party Vegan

Quick-Fix Vegetarian

Vegan Planet

Vegetarian Meat & Potatoes Cookbook

One-Dish Vegetarian

Fresh From the Vegetarian Slow Cooker

Nut Butter Universe

easy vegan recipes
with out-of-this-world flavors

Robin Robertson

Foreword by Julieanna Hever

VEGAN HERITAGE PRESS

Woodstock • Virginia

ISBN 13: 978-0-9800131-7-7
ISBN 10: 0-9800131-7-8

Vegan Heritage Press books are available at quantity discounts. For information, please visit our website at www.veganheritagepress.com or write the publisher at Vegan Heritage Press, P.O. Box 628, Woodstock, VA 22664-0628.

Photography by Lori Maffei. Key to Cover Photos: Front (clockwise from top left) Apple-Almond Butter Pancakes, page 99; Szechuan Stir-Fry with Fiery Peanut Sauce, page 78; Summer Berry Cheesecake, page 110; Stuffed Squash with Brazil Nuts and Pistachios, page 75. Back (left to right) West African Vegetable Stew, page 73; Roasted Sweet Potato Salad with Almond Butter, page 50; Peanut Butter Cups, page 127.

Disclaimer: Allergies to nuts can be a very serious threat to one's health. If you know you have a nut allergy, please take necessary cautions in cooking from this book. If you require a medical diagnosis, or if you are contemplating any major dietary change, consult a qualified health-care provider. You should always seek an expert medical opinion before making changes in your diet or supplementation regimen. The publisher is not responsible for specific health or allergy issues or adverse reactions to recipes contained in this book.

Publisher's Note: The information in this book is correct and complete to the best of our knowledge. Website addresses and contact information were correct at the time of publication.

Library of Congress Cataloging-in-Publication Data

Robertson, Robin (Robin G.)
  [Peanut butter planet]
 Nut butter universe : easy vegan recipes with out-of-this-world flavors / Robin Robertson.
    pages cm
 Includes index.
 "This book is a thorough revision of Peanut Butter Planet: Around the World in 80 Recipes, from Starters to Main Dishes to Desserts by Robin Robertson"
 ISBN-13: 978-0-9800131-7-7
 ISBN-10: 0-9800131-7-8
 1. Cooking (Peanut butter) 2. International cooking. 3. Vegan cooking. I. Title.
 TX814.5.P38R63 2013
 641.6'45--dc23
                    2012041802

Printed in the United States of America

10 9 8 7 6 5 4 3 2 1

Dedication

To my family:
Jon, Gary, Mitzki, Jason, and Peanut

Contents

Foreword

by Julieanna Hever, MS, RD, CPT

I grew up in a completely nut-free household, because my father is allergic to most nuts. We couldn't have nuts anywhere in the house. Once I moved out and was on my own, I slowly began a new journey into an entirely new genre of flavor and texture I had never been privy to. A new world opened up to me as I explored various nuts and nut butters, testing them in recipes and adding them to snacks, recognizing how much I had been missing throughout my youth. Because of my newness to this class of versatile plant-based foods, I am all the more grateful to Robin for creating this gem of a book, enabling me to explore her fresh concepts and ideas, and to indulge in these nutritious and delicious recipes. *Nut Butter Universe* is brimming with creativity, great flavor, and decadence, all the while providing enticing ways to incorporate health-filled nut butters into your daily fare.

Nuts and seeds have been a traditional component of most cultures for millennia. Not only are they delicious and provide delectable additions to a vast variety of dishes, but they also boast extraordinary nutrient profiles and have been associated with multiple health benefits in the scientific literature.

Tree nuts and peanuts (technically a legume masquerading as a nut, thanks to the nomenclature and nutrient profile) are rich in vitamins E, B_6, folate, thiamin, riboflavin, niacin, pantothenic acid, and much-needed minerals like calcium, selenium, iron, zinc, manganese, magnesium, phosphorus, and potassium. They score high on antioxidant ranking systems and provide a plethora of protective phytonutrients. Seeds, too, provide a wealth of nutrients including vitamin E and several from the B complex (namely, thiamine, niacin, folate, and B_6), manganese, tryptophan, calcium, phosphorus, potassium, zinc, and iron. Special super stars of the seed kingdom are sesame seeds and tahini (sesame seed butter) due to their healthy dose of calcium, and chia, flax, and hemp seeds for their abundance of plant-based omega-3 fats.

Although the percentage of calories in nuts and seeds is high in total fat, their fatty acid profile is optimal, made up of primarily monounsaturated fats (although certain nuts like walnuts are predominantly polyunsaturated). Overall, nuts are lower in artery-clogging saturated fats and do not contain nefariously problematic trans fatty acids or dietary cholesterol. Some nuts and seeds are high in the essential polyunsaturated omega-3 fatty acid, alpha-linolenic acid (ALA). In fact, it only takes approximately half a cup of black walnuts, two tablespoons of English walnuts, or one tablespoon of flaxseeds, hemp seeds, or chia seeds to provide the daily Adequate Intake (AI) of ALA. In a vegan diet, these are your best options for attaining your omega-3 fatty acids, and should be considered a consistent component of your meal plan. Robin illustrates some easy and delicious ways of enjoying them throughout this book.

Another unique contribution nuts provide is phytosterols, plant-derived sterols and stanols, which have been associated with cholesterol-optimizing effects as well as lowered risk for certain cancers. Nuts also contain ellagic acid, a potent antioxidant, as well as lignans, which have antioxidant and phytoestrogenic properties. These compounds have been shown to support heart health and protect against certain cancers.

Nuts are an excellent source of healthy plant protein. The biggest benefit of consuming protein from nuts and other plant foods is that it is packaged alongside all of these other wonderful nutrients and yet do not contain harmful steroids, hormones, cholesterol, and saturated fats found in animal products. In fact, the protein content in nuts and seeds helps provide essential amino acids and boost protein intake in a vegan diet. And here is a bonus: L-arginine, one of the amino acids found abundantly in nuts, is the precursor to nitric oxide and its consumption can help improve blood flow by enhancing vasodilation (Brufau, et al, *Brit J Nutr,* 2006). See Chart 1 on page 138 for an illustration of the varied and health-promoting fatty acid profile, and generous fiber and phytosterol content of various nuts and peanuts.

In recent years, research has shed light on numerous compelling benefits of consuming nuts and seeds regularly. Epidemiological data have revealed that nuts appear to reduce your risk of cardiovascular disease, the number one killer of Americans, by approximately one-third or more. The Nurses Health Study is a prospective cohort study that began following 121,700 female nurses in 1976. In a recent analysis (Baer, et al, *Am J Epidemiol* 2011) of the collected data, researchers wanted to assess which lifestyle factors may be associated with mortality. Consuming just two or more servings of nuts per week was found to be associated with lower mortality when compared to women consuming none or almost none. Several studies show a strong cardioprotective effect illustrated by associations between frequent nut consumption and a decreased incidence of mortality, coronary heart disease, myocardial infarction, and sudden cardiac death.

> "Despite the common concerns about the higher fat and calorie content of nuts and seeds, research supports the fact that consuming nuts does not lead to weight gain."

Consuming nuts regularly helps protect against type 2 diabetes. Jiang, et al found a lowered risk for type 2 diabetes with higher nut and peanut butter consumption in women *(JAMA 2002)* while Jenkins, et al, found two ounces of nuts per day in replacement of carbohydrate-rich foods helped improve glycemic control and blood cholesterol in type 2 diabetics *(Diabetes Care 2011).*

Nuts and seeds also improve cholesterol profiles. In a 2005 review (Mukuddem-Petersen, et al, *J Nutr),* it was concluded that consuming 50-100 g (approximately 1.5-3.5 servings) of nuts five or more times a week can decrease total and low-density lipoprotein (LDL) cholesterol levels. A pooled analysis of 25 nut consumption trials (Sabate, et al, *Arch Intern Med,* 2010) determined that eating nuts improves blood cholesterol profiles in a dose-dependent fashion, meaning there is a greater reduction in LDL cholesterol when more calories are replaced by nuts in the diet.

Preliminary evidence supports possible associations between frequent nut consumption and decreased incidence of other chronic diseases such as obesity, dementia, gallstone disease, advanced macular degeneration, and even erectile dysfunction.

Despite the common concerns about the higher fat and calorie content of nuts and seeds, research supports the fact that consuming nuts does not lead to weight gain. In fact, some experts continue the antiquated trend of recommending limiting or excluding them in the diet in order to lose weight or prevent weight gain. However, a comprehensive review in the September 2008 issue of *The Journal of Nutrition* revealed that nuts are not only innocent of the claim they contribute to weight gain, but also that nut consumers tend to have lower body mass indexes (BMIs) than non-consumers. A randomized controlled trial (the gold standard in scientific research) put two groups of obese subjects on a low-calorie diet, where one group consumed 48 almonds a day and the other group had no nuts. At the end of the 18-month trial, both groups lost around the same amount of weight, but the almond-eaters showed significantly greater reductions in total cholesterol and triglycerides levels profiles as well as better total cholesterol to HDL ratios *(Am J Clin Nutr,* 2012).

> "Overall, nuts are lower in artery-clogging saturated fats and do not contain nefariously problematic trans fatty acids or dietary cholesterol."

The key factor is that you need to substitute (instead of adding in additional) calories you were previously consuming to reap the benefits. Adding calories to a diet, regardless of where they are coming from, will lead to weight gain since weight management is simply a physics equation of calories in versus calories out.

Thus, the preponderance of information suggests that consuming a moderate amount of nuts and seeds – approximately one ounce per day – has significant health advantages, particularly when the serving of nuts replaces the calories from somewhere else in the diet.

Nut Butter Universe provides an enchantingly delicious culinary opportunity to indulge in the rich flavors of nut butters, while also boosting your essential nutrient intake and helping reduce the incidence of chronic disease. You can enjoy Robin's enticing and innovative recipes while maintaining your goal for optimal health.

Julieanna Hever, MS, RD, CPT, Plant-Based Dietitian, author of
The Complete Idiot's Guide to Plant-Based Nutrition, and host of
the TV talk show, *What Would Julieanna Do?*

Preface

Nearly a decade ago, I wrote a cookbook of international recipes featuring peanut butter. It was called *Peanut Butter Planet.* Fast forward ten years to find that peanut butter, while still eminently popular and delicious, now shares the culinary stage with several equally fabulous nut and seed butters, such as almond butter, cashew butter, sesame butter, and many more.

Enter **Nut Butter Universe: Easy Vegan Recipes with Out-Of-This-World Flavors,** a complete revision (and reimagining) of my earlier book. **Nut Butter Universe** has been revised, updated, and expanded to contain more than 100 all-vegan recipes that call for a variety of nut and seed butters that can be used in a full range of recipes from starters, soups, and sandwiches, to main dishes, breakfasts, and desserts, with the gluten-free or soy-free recipes clearly marked.

In **Nut Butter Universe,** you'll find many flavor-rich recipes, including: Cream of Chestnut Soup, Roasted Niçoise Salad with Cashew Goddess Dressing, Spinach-Walnut Crostini, Penne Primavera with Avocado Cashew Cream, Apple-Almond Butter Pancakes, and Chocolate-Peanut Butter Cheesecake.

In addition to their deliciousness, nut butters can be a wonderful source of protein and other nutrients. Because of their rich flavors, only a small amount is needed for most recipes. For more information about the healthy benefits of nuts, I encourage you to read the informative Foreword by Julieanna Hever. Of course, if you are allergic to a particular nut, but not others, I'm happy to point out that the various nut and seed butters used in these recipes are virtually interchangeable with each other.

I hope you'll be as excited as I am about my nut butter cookbook, **Nut Butter Universe** – the flavors of these recipes are truly out of this world!

THE NUT BUTTER UNIVERSE

The world of nut butter once revolved around peanut butter alone. But no more. There's a vast universe of new options now available that includes nut butters made from almonds, Brazil nuts, cashews, pistachios, walnuts, and also seeds, such as pumpkin and sunflower. You can even enjoy nut butters with enticing flavor combinations like cinnamon-raisin swirl peanut butter, chocolate sunflower seed almond butter, chocolate hazelnut, vanilla espresso almond butter, and many others (see Make Your Own Flavored Nut Butters on page 105).

Nut butters can be surprisingly versatile ingredients for many recipes and dishes. They add protein and other important nutrients, as well as delicious flavor and a subtle nuttiness that compliments many foods. In addition to providing a basis for many international dishes, nut butters can be used as a replacement for butter, oil, or shortening in baking. They also add wonderful flavor and richness to sauces, gravies, marinades, and dressings. And, of course, they're great on their own or spread on bread for a sandwich.

Easy instructions for making your own nut butters are provided in this book. If you prefer to buy your nut butters off the shelf, there are many sources from which you can buy everything from basic peanut butter and tahini to more exotic nut butters. Look for companies that sell organic nut butters, and be sure the products do not contain hydrogenated fat or other additives. The many varieties can easily be discovered by searching "nut butters" in your favorite search engine.

1 Nuts About Nut Butters

Like most people, my personal nut butter odyssey began in childhood with the frequent appearance of peanut butter and jelly sandwiches in my lunchbox. I never grew tired of them. Whenever my mother prepared something I didn't like for dinner, I always requested one. My love of peanut butter soon extended to sweets, with peanut butter cookies and those decadent chocolate-peanut butter cups topping my list of favorite confections.

Unfortunately, the calorie counting and fat-gram monitoring of adulthood banished my beloved spread to the shelf for a time. As I learned more about international cuisines, however, I discovered that peanut butter is used as a cooking ingredient throughout the world. I soon began looking at my old friend in a new light and realized that because the flavor of peanut butter is so intense, a little goes a long way. Just a small amount is needed to enliven sauces, soups, and other savory dishes.

Around the same time, a wonderful thing happened: medical science revealed that there are "good" fats and "bad" fats. Nut butters were on the list of "good," or monounsaturated, fats. Unlike saturated fats, which can clog the arteries and lead to high cholesterol and heart disease, monounsaturated fats were found to actually help lower cholesterol and improve heart function.

Since then, something equally wonderful has happened: an abundance of delicious, non-peanut, nut and seed butters have become available. This convinced me that a new book on nut and seed butters was in order. I wanted to include all of peanut butter's creamy and delicious friends – the fabulous butters made from almonds, cashews, walnuts, pistachios, pecans, chestnuts, and macadamia nuts, as well as sesame seeds, sunflower seeds, and others.

Peanut Butter: An American Tradition

Peanut butter was first developed in the United States in the 1890s as a high-protein health food. The original patent for peanut butter was given to Dr. John Harvey Kellogg (the Kellogg's cereal magnate) who initially developed peanut butter as a protein alternative for his patients.

> The original patent for peanut butter was given to Dr. John Harvey Kellogg (the cereal magnate) who developed peanut butter as a protein alternative for his patients.

Peanut butter was first introduced to the American public in St. Louis at the 1904 World's Fair, where over $700 worth of it was sold at a penny per sample. Peanut butter has been a favorite kitchen staple in American homes ever since. Commercial production of peanut butter began in earnest in 1908, but the early products had a gritty texture and spoiled easily. That soon changed. In 1922, Joseph L. Rosefield found a way to prevent the oil from separating, and he received the first patent for a shelf-stable peanut butter that stayed fresh for up to a year. Today, of the peanuts grown in the U.S., nearly half are used to make peanut butter. The Jif brand alone is produced at the rate of 250,000 jars per day in the world's largest peanut butter plant in Lexington, Kentucky.

During the twentieth century, peanut butter was used mainly for sandwiches and confections. These days, however, many health-conscious Americans have rediscovered peanut butter as an easy and delicious way to add protein-rich flavor to their meals and a great way to include more "good" fat in their diets.

Some people might dismiss peanut butter as "kid's stuff," but virtually everyone has a jar on hand to appease the child within – whether to make the iconic sandwich or perhaps indulge in one of life's guilty pleasures: dipping a spoon (or finger) directly into the jar at midnight. Peanut butter is convenient and inexpensive, and a nutritional powerhouse rich in protein, fiber, niacin, magnesium, and B vitamins. No wonder peanut butter is America's favorite comfort food! The fact is, we consume nearly 800 million pounds of the creamy spread each year.

Unlike saturated fats, which can clog the arteries and lead to high cholesterol and heart disease, monounsaturated fats were found to actually help lower cholesterol and improve heart function.

Parents turn to peanut butter to nourish fussy kids. Young people and families alike crave it as a delicious and economical protein source, as do the millions of vegans and other health-conscious people. Whether enjoyed as a snack, as part of a meal, or dessert, Americans have a love affair with peanut butter!

"All natural" peanut butter is now commercially available. It is made only from 100 percent peanuts, while "regular," emulsified peanut butter contains added ingredients. The addition of hydrogenated vegetable oil acts as a stabilizer to prevent the oil in the peanut butter from separating, and it gives peanut butter its spreadable consistency. Because hydrogenated oil should be avoided, make every effort to choose a commercial peanut butter that is all natural. Natural or "old-fashioned" style peanut butter contains no stabilizers and often does not contain added sweeteners or salt, and the peanuts used are usually organic. Natural-style peanut butter has a coarser texture and deeper flavor than the commercial brands of regular peanut butter.

Centuries before peanut butter made its first public appearance at the St. Louis World's Fair, it was a staple for the people of Asia, Africa, and South America, who continue to use it in soups, stews, sauces, salads, and main dishes. In fact, over 90 percent of the world's peanuts are grown in Africa and Asia. Peanuts were known as early as 950 BC and originated in South America. The ancient Incas used peanuts, and they are known to have made it into a paste-like substance. As a crop, peanuts emigrated from South America to Africa by early explorers and then traveled by trade into Spain and subsequently to the American colonies.

Nut and Seed Butters Everywhere

The use of nut butters remains common in many countries throughout the world, from the peanut sauces of Thailand to the peanut stews of Africa, as well as sesame dressings of Japan and almond sauces of Spain. In Morocco, almond butter (or "paste") is used to make pastry fillings and other desserts, including a sweet spread known as *amlou,* made with honey and argan oil. Moroccans also combine almond paste with anise, cinnamon, fennel, sesame seeds, oil, honey, and flour to make a sweet and nutritious snack called *sellou.*

Lucky for us in North America, in addition to our beloved peanutty spread, we now have available a wide variety of other nut butters, including almond butter, cashew butter, and seed butters, made with sunflower seeds or pumpkin seeds. Soy nut butter, made from roasted soybeans, is also available. Sesame butters, in the form of tahini and Chinese sesame paste, are also popular in Asian and Middle Eastern cooking. Both sunflower seed butter and soy nut butter are good options for those with peanut or other nut allergies.

> Both sunflower seed butter and soy nut butter are good options for those with peanut or other nut allergies.

We can also find a variety of specialty nut butters, including those that have jelly, chocolate, or flavorings blended right in the jar. In terms of freshness and flavor, however, nothing beats freshly ground nut butters. It is simple to make your own nut butter at home in a high-speed blender or food processor. Recipes for homemade nut butters are provided beginning on page 7.

To Your Health

Nut butters are an excellent source of protein, and they are rich in fiber, vitamins, and essential fatty acids. They are also high in fat, but the fats are mostly unsaturated. Recent medical findings extol the benefits of monounsaturated fats, such as those found in avocados and nut butters. Among other things, these "good" fats have been shown to help reduce high cholesterol, and, because they are low on the glycemic index, nut butters can help control weight gain and diabetes.

> Recent medical findings extol the benefits of monounsaturated fats, such as those found in avocados and nut butters.

In addition to being rich in protein, nut butters are also excellent sources for B-complex vitamins as well as potassium, magnesium, calcium, and iron, making them ideal choices for quality protein and "good" fat. Studies have shown that regularly eating foods rich in unsaturated fat (such as nut butters) can actually help lower blood cholesterol levels. Nut butters are also naturally cholesterol-free.

Because the recipes in this book are free of all animal products, they are accessible not only to vegans but to those who are lactose-intolerant or need to limit their intake of cholesterol and saturated fat. Another thing to keep in mind is that the "per serving" amount of nut butter in most recipes is quite low, so even though many of the recipes may taste decadently rich, they are actually quite healthful.

In addition to being rich in fatty acids, fiber, and phytosterols (see Chart 1 on page 138, nuts are also good sources of protein, calcium, and potassium, and other nutrients (see Chart 2 on page 138).

There are many cases in which particular nuts shine with regard to specific nutrients. For example, Brazil nuts are the highest food source for the essential mineral selenium; sunflower seeds are rich in vitamin E; and cashews are high in iron.

For more detailed information about the many health benefits of nut butters, be sure to read the Foreword by best-selling author Julieanna Hever aka the Plant-Based Dietitian.

Buying and Storing Tips

A variety of nut butters can be found in natural food stores, well-stocked supermarkets, and from several online sources. Natural-style nut butters contain no additives and need to be kept refrigerated to prevent rancidity.

When kept in a tightly sealed jar in the refrigerator, nut butters will keep for several months. Natural nut butters are unprocessed, and the oil and solids sometimes separate in the jar. Just stir them back together before use. Since natural nut butters become stiff when chilled, bring them to room temperature for a few minutes before use to improve spreadability.

Nut Allergies and Alternatives

It is estimated that three million Americans are allergic to peanuts and other nuts. The good news for those afflicted is that the different varieties of nut butters are interchangeable in most of the recipes in this book. If you or someone you cook for are allergic to peanuts (but not other nuts), simply substitute another variety of nut butter for peanut butter in the recipes.

Likewise, if you have sensitivity to another nut (or simply prefer certain nuts over others) feel free to use whatever nut butter you prefer in any of the recipes in this book. Typically, sunflower seed butter or soy nut butter are delicious alternatives to nut butters for those who have allergies. (See specific information on soy and gluten sensitivities on page 12.)

Commercial vs. Homemade

For convenience, you can use commercial nut butters in any of the recipes in this book. Homemade nut butters, however, are superior in flavor and can be more economical. In addition, most commercial nut butters (other than peanut butter) can be expensive and more difficult to find. It may, therefore, prove more economical (and flavorful) to make your own. Just be sure to make them in small batches, as fresh-ground nut butter is more perishable than commercial varieties.

It bears repeating that homemade butters should also be stored in the refrigerator in a tightly covered container (a small wide-mouth jar with a tight-fitting lid is perfect) where they will keep for up to a month. For easier spreading, nut butters should be brought to room temperature before using them in a recipe.

Generally, there is a 2-to-1 ratio of nuts used to the nut butter yield (for example, 1 cup of nuts makes approximately 1/2 cup of nut butter).

Making Your Own Nut Butters

Making your own nut butters at home is as simple as grinding nuts in a food processor until they form a paste. Grinding your own nut butters can actually be a gratifying experience. The results taste fresh and delicious and can be more economical than buying commercial nut butters. On the next page is a basic recipe for homemade nut butter made in a food processor. Nut butters can also be made in a blender, but they can be more difficult to manage because it takes more effort to keep scraping them down from the sides and bottom of a blender than it does in a food processor.

To Roast or Not to Roast?

The choice to roast nuts used for making nut butter is a matter of personal preference. Raw foodists wouldn't consider it, but some nuts, such as walnuts, can be bitter when raw, and the roasting process removes any bitterness. Roasted nuts add more depth of flavor to nut butters. To me, roasted nut butters taste like an intense, creamy version of the nut from which it was made.

To roast nuts, preheat the oven to 375° F. Spread the raw nuts on a baking sheet and roast for 10 to 12 minutes, stirring a couple of times to prevent burning. They should be fragrant and lightly browned. Remove from the oven and transfer to a plate or shallow bowl to cool.

Roasted nut butter can take up to 12 to 15 minutes to make in a food processor, depending on the nut. A small amount of oil, such as coconut oil or neutral vegetable oil, may be added when making butter using harder, drier, or older nuts.

Basic Nut Butter

Makes 1 cup

This basic recipe calls for roasted nuts because they have more flavor and roasting helps bring out the oils. You can also use raw or soaked nuts if you prefer. This recipe can also be used for shelled sunflower or pumpkin seeds.

    2 cups roasted shelled nuts (any variety)
    1 tablespoon neutral vegetable oil (optional)
    1/4 teaspoon salt, or to taste (omit if salted nuts are used)

Place the nuts, oil (if using), and salt (if using), in a food processor with the metal "S" blade and process for 2 to 3 minutes. Stop to scrape down the sides of container with a rubber spatula and continue to process until the desired consistency is reached, 10 to 15 minutes total, depending on the nuts used.

Transfer to a tightly covered container, and store in the refrigerator. For a more spreadable consistency, remove from the refrigerator about 20 minutes before using. If the oil rises to the top, stir before using.

Nut Creams

Nut butters are easy to transform into nut creams and used to make rich sauces for savory and sweet recipes. To make a nut cream, whisk up to 1 cup of water (or other liquid, depending on the recipe) into 1/4 cup of nut butter until smooth. The most widely used nut cream is made with neutral-flavored cashew butter, with almond butter a close second. More boldly-flavored nut creams, such as walnut cream, make a flavorful sauce for pasta.

Nut-Based Dairy-Free Basics

A number of basic ingredients called for in this book, such as dairy-free mayonnaise, sour cream, and cream cheese, can be made with nut butters. You can certainly buy prepared versions of these ingredients, if you prefer, or you can make them yourself using these recipes.

Cashew Sour Cream

Makes 1 cup

3/4 cup raw cashews, soaked 3 hours or overnight, and drained
1/3 cup plain unsweetened almond milk
2 tablespoons lemon juice
1/4 teaspoon salt

Grind the cashews to a powder in a high-speed blender. Add the remaining ingredients and process until very smooth, scraping the container as needed. Transfer to a clean jar, cover tightly, and refrigerate until needed.

Cashew Cream Cheese

Makes about 2 cups

3/4 cup raw cashews
1 (12-ounce) box extra-firm silken tofu
1 1/2 tablespoons lemon juice
Pinch salt

Grind the cashews in a high-speed blender until finely ground. Add the remaining ingredients and process until very smooth, scraping down as needed. Transfer to a clean jar, cover tightly, and refrigerate until needed.

Cashew Mayo

Makes about 1 cup

3/4 cup soaked raw cashews, soaked 3 hours or overnight and drained
1/4 cup plain unsweetened almond milk
1 tablespoon unseasoned rice vinegar
1 teaspoon lemon juice
1/2 teaspoon salt
1/4 teaspoon dry mustard
1/4 cup water

Grind the cashews in a high-speed blender until finely ground. Add the remaining ingredients and process until very smooth, scraping down as needed. Transfer to a clean jar, cover tightly, and refrigerate until needed.

Nutty Parmesan

Makes about 3/4 cup

3/4 cup raw nuts of choice
1/4 to 1/3 cup nutritional yeast
1/2 teaspoon salt

Combine the ingredients in a food processor and process until finely ground. Transfer to a tightly covered container, and store in the refrigerator.

Nut Cheese Sauce

Makes about 1 1/2 cups

3 tablespoons nutritional yeast
2 tablespoons almond butter
1 tablespoon tahini
1 tablespoon white miso paste
1 tablespoon cornstarch
1 tablespoon lemon juice
1/4 teaspoon salt
1 cup almond milk

Combine all of the ingredients in a blender or food processor, and process until very smooth. Transfer the mixture to a small saucepan over medium heat. Stir for a few minutes until it starts to thicken, then remove from the heat. It is now ready to serve.

Seed Butters

Delicious "butters" can also be made of certain seeds. Those used in this book, pumpkin and sunflower seed butter, can be made using the nut butter recipe above, however, there are a few exceptions where a slightly different recipe is in order. One such exception is sesame butter.

Two Kinds of Sesame Butter

It's important to note that not all sesame butters are created equal. Chinese sesame paste, for example, is made from *roasted* sesame seeds, while Middle Eastern sesame butter, known as tahini, is made from *unroasted* sesame seeds and is sometimes thinned with olive oil. Chinese sesame paste, used in Asian recipes such as stir-fries and sauces, is denser in texture and richer in flavor than tahini. Tahini is used to make hummus, baba ghanoush, and other Middle Eastern recipes. Both Chinese sesame paste and tahini are available in well-stocked supermarkets or ethnic grocery stores.

Because of the difference in flavor and texture, I am providing two recipes for sesame butter, one made with raw sesame seeds and the other made with toasted sesame seeds.

Raw Sesame Butter (Tahini)

Makes 1 cup

This recipe will result in a sesame butter that is similar to commercial tahini. Soaking the sesame seeds will soften them and make a smoother butter.

1/2 cup sesame seeds (soaked 4 hours or overnight)
1 tablespoon olive oil
1/8 teaspoon salt (optional)
1/2 cup warm water, as needed

Drain the sesame seeds well, then transfer them to a high-speed blender or food processor and grind until smooth. Add the olive oil and salt, if using. Process until combined. With the motor running, add some of the water in a slow, steady stream and blend until smooth, adding as much of the water as needed to achieve the desired consistency. Transfer to a bowl or jar, cover tightly, and store in the refrigerator.

Toasted Sesame Butter

Makes 1 cup

The end result of this recipe will be similar to commercial Chinese sesame paste — thicker and more deeply flavored than tahini.

1 cup sesame seeds
1 tablespoon dark sesame oil
1/8 teaspoon salt (optional)
1/4 cup water, if needed

Heat a large skillet over medium-high heat. Add the sesame seeds and toast lightly for about 2 minutes, stirring continually so they toast evenly. Watch carefully so the seeds do not burn — it can happen quickly. As soon as they start to turn golden brown, they are ready.

Transfer the toasted seeds to a bowl and set aside to cool completely.

Transfer the cooled toasted seeds to a food processor or high-speed blender. Add the sesame oil and salt, if using, and pulse for 3 to 4 minutes, or until smooth, scraping down the sides as needed. Add a little more oil or some water, if needed, to achieve the desired consistency. Transfer to a bowl or jar, cover tightly, and store in the refrigerator.

Cooking with Nut and Seed Butters

It's easy to incorporate nut and seed butters into our diets for their protein content and other health benefits, as well as for their rich, dreamy flavors. Easy-to-make, fresh nut butters add complexity and depth to both sweet and savory dishes. Among other things, they can be used to flavor, thicken, and replace dairy cream in traditional recipes.

From the spicy Asian sauces and hearty African stews, this book provides nut butter recipes for everything from appetizers to exotic sauces and soups, to main dishes. As the more than 100 sumptuous recipes in this book will attest, nut butters have come of age, and can take us for a delicious gustatory ride.

Serving Yields

Most of the recipes in this book yield four servings. However, the supplied yield amounts are a guideline and not a hard-and-fast rule. We don't all eat the same amount at meals – some people have large appetites while others prefer smaller portions. The recipes also may be served alone or with other dishes. If your family prefers smaller portions, or if you plan to serve a few other dishes with a particular recipe, then you may be able to get additional portions out of a recipe.

Options: Gluten-Free, Soy-Free, No Added Oil

Many people today seek recipes that are gluten-free, soy-free, or low in fat, so it was important to me while I developed these recipes to make them accessible to as many people as possible, regardless of any dietary restrictions. For that reason, most of the recipes are naturally low in added oil. For example, in many cases, a choice is given to sauté ingredients either in water or in a small amount of oil.

Many of the recipes are also either gluten-free, soy-free, or both, and they are noted with each recipe for quick reference. Wherever possible, easy substitutions are given to make a recipe either gluten-free or soy-free. For example, you may substitute gluten-free pasta for regular pasta or lima beans for edamame.

In this book, gluten-free or soy-free recipes are noted as follows:

- Gluten Free
- Soy Free

When recipes can easily be made gluten-free or soy-free with a simple substitution, they are listed as Gluten-Free Option or Soy-Free Option.

If You Have Sensitivity to Gluten

Recipes that are marked "gluten-free" do not contain common gluten ingredients such as seitan, wheat, barley, or rye. Such recipes will call for gluten-free oats or wheat-free tamari (I always use wheat-free tamari). However, just as hidden animal ingredients can find their way into certain products, so too is the case with gluten and soy, so you need to maintain your own vigilance with regards to trace ingredients that may be in the particular products you buy.

IF YOU HAVE SENSITIVITY TO GLUTEN

If you have a serious gluten or soy sensitivity, read *all* labels carefully to be sure the products you are buying are gluten-free or soy-free. For example, certain commercially available products, such as hoisin sauce, and commercial vegetable broth, soup base paste, and bouillon cubes may contain gluten, although gluten-free versions are easily found in most markets. Many commercial sauces and condiments (i.e., mustard, ketchup, etc.) are typically gluten-free and soy-free, but check labels to be sure they contain no gluten or soy. For information regarding gluten-free ingredients, visit www.celiac.com. Naturally, the same cautionary advice is true for soy and other food allergies you may have. (See nut allergy page 5.)

2 Soups

Peruvian Peanut Potato Soup

Serves 6

1 tablespoon neutral vegetable oil or 1/4 cup water
1 large yellow onion, chopped
1 pound all-purpose potatoes, peeled and diced
6 cups vegetable broth
2/3 cup peanut butter (page 7)
Salt and ground black pepper
1 tablespoon chopped chives

The peanut plant is believed to have originated in South America. Records show that the Incas of Peru used peanuts as sacrificial offerings and entombed them with their mummies as early as 1500 BC. Since both peanuts and potatoes are Peruvian crops, they are combined in this flavorful soup. There are two ways to serve this soup. Served chunky, it is homey and rustic, and is especially good served with coarse dark bread. Puree the soup and it turns a lovely butterscotch color and looks quite elegant, especially garnished with chives.

Heat the oil or water in a large pot over medium heat. Add the onion, cover, and cook until softened, about 5 minutes. Add the potatoes and broth, and cook until the potatoes are tender, about 40 minutes. Stir in the peanut butter, and season with salt and pepper to taste.

If a chunky soup is desired, it can be served at this point, garnished with the chives.

For a smooth soup, puree the mixture in a blender or food processor until smooth, or use an immersion blender to puree the soup right in the pot.

Return the soup to the pot and heat over medium heat until hot, about 5 minutes. Serve garnished with the chives.

Curried Almond Sweet Potato Soup

This soup has it all: great taste, vibrant color, and the creamy goodness of almond butter. For this recipe, I use Frontier brand organic curry powder, a heady blend of coriander, turmeric, cumin, mustard, fenugreek, cardamom, nutmeg, red pepper, cinnamon, and cloves, but most any curry spice blend should perform well. For a thinner soup, stir in a small amount of nondairy milk during the final heating.

Heat the oil or water in a large pot over medium heat. Add the onion and garlic, cover, and cook until softened, about 5 minutes.

Add the tomatoes, broth, and sweet potatoes. Bring to a boil, then reduce the heat to low. Cook, uncovered, until the potatoes are soft, about 30 minutes.

Stir in the almond butter, curry powder, cayenne, and salt to taste. Remove from the heat and allow to cool.

Puree the mixture in a blender or food processor until smooth, or use an immersion blender to puree the soup right in the pot. Heat the soup over low heat until hot. Serve sprinkled with the chopped almonds.

Gluten Free
Soy Free

Serves 4 to 6

1 tablespoon neutral vegetable oil or 1/4 cup water
1 large yellow onion, chopped
1 clove garlic, chopped
1 (28-ounce) can crushed tomatoes
5 cups vegetable broth or water
2 large sweet potatoes, peeled and cut into 1-inch chunks
2/3 cup almond butter (page 7)
1 tablespoon curry powder
1/4 teaspoon cayenne pepper
Salt
1/4 cup chopped roasted almonds

African Peanut Soup

Gluten Free
Soy Free

Serves 6

1 tablespoon neutral vegetable oil
  or 1/4 cup water
1 large yellow onion, chopped
1 large red bell pepper, diced
2 cloves garlic, chopped
1 (28-ounce) can diced tomatoes,
  undrained
5 cups vegetable broth
1/2 cup brown rice
1/2 teaspoon red pepper flakes
Salt and ground black pepper
2/3 cup peanut butter (page 7)
2 tablespoons chopped roasted
  peanuts

Because peanuts are an abundant crop in Africa and a good, inexpensive source of protein, peanut soup can be found in many African countries. Traditionally, African peanut soups begin with whole peanuts that are ground to a paste, but beginning with peanut butter is infinitely more convenient.

Heat the oil or water in a large pot over medium heat. Add the onion, bell pepper, and garlic. Cover and cook until softened, about 5 minutes.

Stir in the tomatoes, their juice, and the broth. Bring to a boil. Add the rice, red pepper flakes, and salt and pepper to taste. Reduce the heat to low and simmer, partially covered, until the rice is tender, about 40 minutes.

Ladle about 1 cup of broth into a small bowl, add the peanut butter, and stir until smooth. Stir the peanut butter mixture back into the soup until it is incorporated. Serve hot, sprinkled with the chopped peanuts.

EASY NUT BUTTER SOUP

Combine two parts vegetable broth with one part nut butter (any kind) in a saucepan. Simmer for 15 minutes over medium heat, stirring until smooth and well blended. Season with salt and black pepper, to taste. Stir in a splash of almond milk before serving, if desired. Garnish with chopped nuts.

Cheesy Almond Broccoli Soup

Just as you don't need dairy cream to have a creamy soup, you don't need dairy cheese to add a cheesy flavor to recipes. Almond butter adds extra richness to this flavorful soup.

In a large pot, heat the oil or water over medium heat. Add the onion, cover, and cook until softened, about 5 minutes. Add the potato and broccoli, and stir in the broth. Season with salt and pepper, to taste. Bring to a boil, then reduce the heat to low. Simmer, uncovered, until the vegetables are tender, about 20 minutes. Use a slotted spoon to remove 1/2 cup of small broccoli florets, and set aside.

Add the nutritional yeast, almond butter, lemon juice, and mustard to the soup.

Use an immersion blender to puree the soup directly in the pot, or transfer to a high-speed blender or food processor and puree, in batches if necessary, then return to the pot.

Stir in the almond milk, then taste and adjust the seasonings, if necessary. Reheat the soup over low heat until hot. To serve, ladle soup into bowls, garnish with the reserved broccoli florets. Serve hot.

Gluten Free
Soy Free

Serves 4 to 6

1 tablespoon olive oil or 1/4 cup water

1 medium yellow onion, coarsely chopped

1 medium russet potato, peeled and finely chopped or shredded

1 pound broccoli, trimmed and coarsely chopped

3 cups vegetable broth

Salt and ground black pepper

1/2 cup nutritional yeast

1/4 cup almond butter (page 7)

1 tablespoon lemon juice

1 teaspoon Dijon mustard

2 cups plain unsweetened almond milk

Pumpkin-Pecan Soup with Pecan Butter Croutons

Soy Free
Gluten-Free Option

Serves 6

SOUP:
1 tablespoon olive oil or 1/4 cup water
1 large yellow onion, chopped
1 clove garlic, minced
1/2 red or yellow bell pepper, chopped
1 small hot chile, seeded and minced (optional)
1 (14.5-ounce) can diced tomatoes, undrained
1 (16-ounce) can solid-pack pumpkin
4 cups vegetable broth
1/4 teaspoon dried thyme
Salt and ground black pepper
2/3 cup pecan butter (page 7)

CROUTONS:
2 tablespoons pecan butter (page 7)
1 tablespoon neutral vegetable oil
3 to 4 slices firm white bread

A fresh pumpkin or orange-fleshed winter squash may be used instead of the canned pumpkin. To do so, peel and seed the pumpkin or squash. Cut it into 1/2-inch chunks. Add to the pot with the onion, and proceed. The hot chile may be omitted for those who prefer a mild soup. To make this gluten-free, use a gluten-free bread for the croutons.

SOUP: Heat the oil or water in a large pot over medium heat. Add the onion, garlic, bell pepper, and chile, if using. Cover and cook until softened, stirring occasionally, about 5 minutes.

Stir in the tomatoes, pumpkin, broth, thyme, and salt and pepper to taste. Bring to a boil, then reduce the heat to low, cover, and simmer for 45 minutes.

Stir in the pecan butter. Puree the mixture in a blender or food processor until smooth, or use an immersion blender to puree the soup right in the pot. Simmer the soup 10 to 15 minutes longer. Taste to adjust the seasonings.

CROUTONS: Preheat the oven to 400°F. Lightly oil a 10 x 15-inch baking pan and set aside.

In a small bowl, combine the pecan butter and oil, and blend until smooth.

Place a sheet of wax paper on a cutting board. Brush both sides of the bread slices with the pecan butter mixture, and place on the wax paper. Cut each slice of bread lengthwise into 1/2-inch strips, then cut the slices crosswise to form the croutons.

Separate the croutons and transfer them to the prepared pan. Bake until browned, stirring occasionally, about 8 minutes. Cool completely before using to garnish the soup. Store in an airtight container.

Artichoke-Walnut Butter Bisque

Walnut butter adds buttery rich counterpoint to the artichokes in this elegant soup. Frozen artichoke hearts are used because they are superior in flavor to canned, and they don't have the expense or labor of fresh ones.

In a large pot, heat the oil or water over medium heat. Add the shallots, cover, and cook until softened. Uncover and stir in the artichoke hearts, broth, and salt, to taste. Bring to a boil, then reduce heat to low. Simmer, uncovered, until the artichokes are tender, 15 to 20 minutes.

Stir in the walnut butter, lemon juice, and cayenne. Use an immersion blender to puree the soup right in the pot, or transfer the soup to a high-speed blender or food processor, in batches if necessary, and puree. Return the soup to the pot. Stir in the almond milk, then taste and adjust the seasonings, if necessary, adding more salt if needed. Simmer the soup over medium heat until hot, about 5 minutes.

Ladle into 4 bowls, top with the marinated artichokes, then sprinkle with the chives and walnuts, and serve hot.

Gluten Free
Soy Free

Serves 4

1 tablespoon olive oil or 1/4 cup water

1 large or 2 small shallots, chopped

2 (10-ounce) packages frozen artichoke hearts, thawed

3 cups vegetable broth

Salt

1/3 cup walnut butter (page 7)

2 teaspoons fresh lemon juice

1/8 teaspoon ground cayenne

1 cup plain unsweetened almond milk

1 (6-ounce) jar marinated artichokes, drained and chopped or thinly sliced

1 tablespoon snipped fresh chives, for garnish

2 tablespoons chopped toasted walnuts, for garnish

Cream of Chestnut Soup

Gluten Free
Soy Free

Serves 4

1 tablespoon olive oil or 1/4 cup water
1 yellow onion, coarsely chopped
1 carrot, coarsely chopped
1 celery rib, coarsely chopped
12 ounces cooked and peeled chestnuts
4 cups vegetable broth
3 tablespoons chopped fresh parsley
1/4 teaspoon ground allspice
1/4 teaspoon ground ginger
1/8 teaspoon cayenne
1 bay leaf
Salt
1/2 cup plain unsweetened almond milk

This rich, opulent bisque is a wonderful first course for a special autumn or winter meal, especially Thanksgiving or Christmas. Since fresh chestnuts can be difficult to find and time consuming to prepare, I stock up on frozen or jarred chestnuts whenever I find them on sale. The least expensive prepared chestnuts can be found in vacuum-packed bags in Asian markets.

In a large pot, heat the oil or water over medium heat. Add the onion, carrot, and celery. Cover and cook until the vegetables are softened, about 10 minutes.

Thinly slice 3 of the chestnuts and set them aside for garnish. Add the remaining chestnuts to the saucepan, along with the broth, parsley, allspice, ginger, cayenne, bay leaf, and salt, to taste. Bring to a boil, then reduce heat to low and simmer, covered, for 30 minutes.

Remove the bay leaf and discard. Use an immersion blender to puree the soup directly in the pot or transfer to a high-speed blender or food processor and puree it in batches if necessary, then return the soup to the pot.

Stir in the almond milk, and taste and adjust the seasonings, if necessary. Reheat over medium heat until hot. To serve, ladle the soup into 4 bowls, garnish with the sliced chestnuts, and serve hot.

Southern Peanut Soup

Many cooks throughout the South have their own version of peanut soup. These soups all have one thing in common: the rich creamy taste of peanut butter. If a thinner consistency is desired, stir in a little additional broth just before serving.

Heat the oil or water in a large pot over medium heat. Add the onion and celery, cover, and cook until softened, about 5 minutes. Add the potato and broth, and bring to a boil. Reduce the heat to low and simmer uncovered until the vegetables are tender, about 30 minutes.

Remove the soup from the heat. Puree the mixture in a blender or food processor until smooth, or use an immersion blender to puree the soup right in the pot. Return all but 1 cup of the soup to the pot, and return to a simmer.

Add the peanut butter to the reserved cup of soup, and puree until smooth. Stir the peanut butter mixture into the soup. Taste the soup before seasoning with salt and pepper – the amount of salt needed will depend upon the saltiness of your broth and peanut butter. Simmer for 10 minutes to blend flavors. To serve, ladle the soup into bowls and sprinkle with the chopped peanuts.

Gluten Free
Soy Free

Serves 6

1 tablespoon olive oil or 1/4 cup water
1 yellow onion, chopped
1 rib celery, chopped
1 large baking potato, peeled and chopped
5 cups vegetable broth
3/4 cup peanut butter (page 7)
Salt and ground black pepper
1/4 cup chopped roasted peanuts

Curried Cashew Vegetable Soup

Serves 6

1 1/2 tablespoons neutral-flavored
  vegetable oil
2 large onions, chopped
3 to 4 cloves garlic, minced
1 large celery stalk, diced
1 cup cashew butter (page 7)
2 teaspoons minced fresh ginger,
  or to taste
2 teaspoons good-quality curry
  powder, more or less to taste
1 teaspoon ground cumin
Pinch of nutmeg
1 tablespoon lemon juice, or more
  to taste
1/2 cup orange juice, preferably
  fresh
3 cups steamed fresh green vegetables (such as finely chopped
  broccoli, green peas, diced zucchini, cut green beans, or any
  combination)
Salt and ground pepper to taste
Thinly sliced scallions for garnish
Chopped cashews for garnish,
  optional

Cashews make an unusual and rich-tasting base for a soup. With notes of ginger, curry, and citrus, this soup is good hot or at room temperature. This recipe is from Nava Atlas, author of numerous cookbooks and editor of the popular web site VegKitchen.com.

Heat the oil in a soup pot. Add the onions, garlic, and celery and sauté over medium-low heat until all are lightly browned. Transfer to a food processor with 1 cup water and process until smoothly pureed, then transfer to the soup pot. Or, simply add 1 cup water to the pot and process with an immersion blender until pureed.

Add 3 cups water and bring to a rapid simmer. Whisk in the cashew butter, about 1/3 cup at a time. Stir in the ginger, curry powder, cumin, nutmeg, lemon juice, and orange juice. Bring to a rapid simmer, then lower the heat. Cover and simmer gently for 15 minutes.

Stir in the steamed vegetables. The soup should have a slightly thick consistency. If the soup is too thick, add a bit more water. Season with salt and pepper, then serve. Garnish each serving with a sprinkling of scallion and, if desired, a few chopped cashews.

Creamy Mushroom Soup

For the creamiest texture, you can puree this delicious soup in a high-speed blender. If using a regular blender or food processor, strain the soup through a fine-mesh sieve before serving.

In a large soup pot, heat the oil or water over medium heat. Add the onion and celery, cover, and cook until softened, about 5 minutes. Add the mushrooms and cook, stirring, 1 minute longer. Stir in the broth and thyme, then add salt and pepper, to taste (how much salt you add depends on the saltiness of your broth). Bring to a boil, then reduce the heat to low and simmer, uncovered, until the vegetables are tender, about 20 minutes.

Add the almond butter. Puree the soup in the pot with an immersion blender, or transfer to a high-speed blender or food processor, in batches if necessary, and puree, then return to the pot. Stir in the almond milk, then taste and adjust the seasonings, if necessary. Reheat the soup over low heat until hot.

Ladle soup into bowls, garnish with the parsley and toasted almonds. Serve hot.

Gluten Free
Soy Free

Serves 4

- 1 tablespoon olive oil or 1/4 cup water
- 1 medium yellow onion, coarsely chopped
- 1 celery rib, coarsely chopped
- 8 ounces white mushrooms, lightly rinsed, patted dry, and quartered
- 8 ounces cremini mushrooms, lightly rinsed, patted dry, and quartered
- 5 cups vegetable broth, mushroom broth, or water
- 1 teaspoon minced fresh thyme or 1/2 teaspoon dried
- Salt and ground black pepper
- 3 tablespoons almond butter (page 7)
- 1 cup plain unsweetened almond milk
- 2 tablespoons minced fresh parsley
- 2 tablespoons toasted sliced almonds

Indonesian-Inspired Coconut-Peanut Soup

Serves 4

1 tablespoon neutral vegetable oil
  or 1/4 cup water
3 shallots, chopped
1 medium carrot, chopped
1 clove garlic, crushed
1 small hot chile, seeded and
  minced (optional)
1 teaspoon minced fresh ginger
1 (14.5-ounce) can diced tomatoes, undrained
3 cups vegetable broth
1 teaspoon natural sugar
1/4 teaspoon cayenne
Salt and ground black pepper
2/3 cup peanut butter (page 7)
1 cup unsweetened coconut milk
2 teaspoons fresh lime juice
1/2 cup fresh bean sprouts,
  blanched
1/4 cup crushed roasted peanuts
2 tablespoons minced fresh cilantro leaves

The intense, vibrant flavors of Indonesia are the inspiration for this creamy soup redolent of ginger, lime juice, coconut, cilantro, and of course, peanut butter — all in a wonderful balance that is right on target. The bean sprouts add a nice crunch, while the cilantro adds a lovely color contrast to the pale orange soup. Blanch the bean sprouts for 30 seconds — just long enough to remove the raw taste.

Heat the oil or water in a large pot over medium heat. Add the shallots and carrot, cover, and cook until softened, about 5 minutes.

Add the garlic, chile (if using), ginger, tomatoes, broth, sugar, cayenne, and salt and pepper to taste. Bring to a boil, then reduce the heat to low and simmer until the vegetables are tender, about 20 minutes. Stir in the peanut butter and remove from the heat.

Puree the mixture in a blender or food processor until smooth, or use an immersion blender to puree the soup right in the pot.

Return to the saucepan, stir in the coconut milk and lime juice, and simmer until hot. Taste and adjust the seasonings, if needed. Serve garnished with bean sprouts, peanuts, and cilantro.

Carrot-Cashew Soup with Apple

This bright and versatile soup can be served piping hot in cold weather, but is also refreshingly delicious when served cold. I like to use a tart Granny Smith apple, but a sweeter variety such as Fuji or Gala may be used.

Heat the oil or water in a large pot over medium heat. Add the onion, carrots, celery, and potato. Cover and cook, stirring occasionally, until the vegetables are softened. Add the apple, ginger, cinnamon, broth or water, apple juice, and salt and pepper to taste. Cover and bring to a boil. Reduce the heat and simmer until the vegetables are tender, 20 to 30 minutes. Stir in the cashew butter.

Puree the mixture in a blender or food processor until smooth, or use an immersion blender to puree the soup right in the pot.

Pour the soup back into the pot and heat until hot. If serving cold, pour the soup into a container and refrigerate until chilled. Serve garnished with apple slices and chopped cashews.

Gluten Free
Soy Free

Serves 6

1 tablespoon neutral vegetable oil or 1/4 cup water
1 yellow onion, diced
1 pound carrots, peeled and chopped
1 rib celery, chopped
1 baking potato, peeled and chopped
1 large cooking apple, peeled, cut in chunks
2 teaspoons minced fresh ginger
1/4 teaspoon cinnamon
3 cups vegetable broth or water
1 cup apple juice
Salt and ground black pepper
1/3 cup cashew butter (page 7)
1 small apple, unpeeled, thinly sliced
2 tablespoons chopped roasted cashews

3 Starters

Smoke and Spice Almond Hummus

Makes about 2 cups

2 garlic cloves, crushed
1 1/2 cups or 1 (15.5-ounce) can chickpeas, rinsed and drained
1 or 2 chipotle chiles in adobo sauce
2 oil-packed or rehydrated sun-dried tomatoes, drained
3 tablespoons almond butter (page 7)
2 tablespoons lime juice
1 teaspoon smoked paprika
1/2 teaspoon ground coriander
1/2 teaspoon cumin
1/4 cup plus 1 tablespoon water
Salt and ground black pepper
3 tablespoons chopped cilantro
1/2 cup roasted slivered almonds, for garnish

Chipotle chiles and smoked paprika provide a smoky heat, while sun-dried tomatoes, lime juice, and a variety of seasonings add to the intriguing flavor palate of this bold dip.

In a food processor, combine the garlic, chickpeas, chipotle, and tomatoes, and process to a paste. Add the almond butter, lime juice, paprika, coriander, cumin, and the water.

Process until smooth and creamy. Season with salt and pepper to taste, and add 2 tablespoons of the cilantro. Pulse to combine thoroughly.

Transfer the hummus to a bowl. If not serving right away, cover and refrigerate until needed.

If serving right away, sprinkle the top with the almonds and remaining cilantro.

NUTS IN HISTORY

In a 13th century Arabic cookbook, tahini is listed as a recipe ingredient.

Crudité with Spicy Cashew Dip

Choose your favorite assortment of raw and blanched vegetables, cut into sticks, slices, florets, or other appropriate shapes. Arrange them on a platter, add the dip, and you have a party! The vegetables used here can be swapped for others of your own preference. To make this soy-free, use coconut aminos instead of the tamari.

DIP: Combine the cashew butter, jam, ginger, garlic, lime juice, tamari, and cayenne in a small bowl. Stir until thoroughly blended. A small amount of water may be added if a thinner consistency is desired.

Transfer the dip to a small serving bowl and place it in the center of a serving tray or platter.

VEGETABLES: Arrange all the vegetables on the serving tray in a decorative fashion, surrounding the bowl of dip. Serve at once, or cover and refrigerate until ready to serve.

Gluten Free
Soy-Free Option

Serves 6

DIP:
1/4 cup cashew butter (page 7)
1/4 cup peach or apricot jam
1 teaspoon grated fresh ginger
1/2 teaspoon minced garlic
1 tablespoon lime juice
1 tablespoon wheat-free tamari
1/8 teaspoon cayenne, or to taste

VEGETABLES:
2 large carrots, peeled and cut into
    1/4-inch x 4-inch sticks
2 ounces snow peas, ends trimmed
    and tough string removed
3 ribs celery, trimmed and cut into
    1/4-inch x 4-inch sticks
1 large red or yellow bell pepper,
    seeded and cut into 1/4-inch
    strips
1 head Belgian endive, trimmed

Spinach-Artichoke Almond Dip

Gluten Free
Soy Free

Makes about 3 1/2 cups

1 tablespoon olive oil or 1/4 cup water
1 small yellow onion, chopped
2 garlic cloves, minced
8 ounces fresh baby spinach
1 1/2 cups canned, marinated, or cooked frozen artichoke hearts, drained
1 cup cooked white beans
1/3 cup almond butter (page 7)
1/3 cup nutritional yeast
1 1/2 tablespoons fresh lemon juice
1/2 teaspoon Tabasco sauce
1 teaspoon salt
1/4 teaspoon black pepper

Almond butter adds richness to this addictively delicious dip. Serve with your favorite crackers or chips, or with lightly toasted baguette slices or raw veggies.

Preheat the oven to 350°F. Lightly oil a small baking dish or spray it with cooking spray. Set aside.

Heat the oil or water in a large skillet over medium heat. Add the onion and cook until softened, about 4 minutes. Add the garlic and cook 1 minute longer. Add the spinach, stirring to wilt. Once the spinach is wilted, remove from the heat.

Coarsely chop the artichokes and add to the spinach mixture. Set aside.

In a food processor, combine the beans, almond butter, nutritional yeast, lemon juice, Tabasco, salt, and pepper; process until smooth and creamy. Add the reserved spinach and artichokes and pulse to combine, leaving some texture. Taste and adjust the seasonings, adding more salt or lemon juice, if needed.

Transfer the mixture into the prepared baking dish. Bake until heated through, about 25 minutes. Serve with dippers of choice.

Sriracha-Spiked Hummus

This popular protein-rich dip is enlivened by a jolt of sriracha. For a kid-friendly version, you can omit the sriracha. For a slightly different flavor experience, substitute peanut butter or another nut butter for the tahini.

Puree the chickpeas and garlic, in a food processor until smooth. Add the tahini, lemon juice, sriracha, and salt. Process until smooth and well blended. Add some water if a thinner consistency is desired.

Transfer to a tightly covered container and refrigerate for at least an hour before serving to allow flavors to develop.

Serve chilled or at room temperature topped with a sprinkling of parsley.

Gluten Free
Soy Free

Makes about 2 cups

1 1/2 cups cooked or 1 (15.5-ounce) can chickpeas, drained and rinsed
1 large clove garlic, chopped
1/4 cup tahini or sesame butter (page 8)
2 tablespoons fresh lemon juice
1 to 2 teaspoons sriracha sauce
1/2 teaspoon salt
Water, as needed
1 tablespoon minced fresh parsley or cilantro

NUTS IN HISTORY

Herodotus wrote about the cultivation of sesame seeds 3,500 years ago near the Tigris and Euphrates rivers.

Asian Spring Rolls with Spicy Peanut Dipping Sauce

Gluten Free
Soy-Free Option

Serves 4

SAUCE:

1/4 cup peanut butter (page 7)

2 tablespoons wheat-free tamari

1/4 cup water

1 tablespoon rice vinegar

1 tablespoon fresh lime juice

1 teaspoon finely minced garlic

1 teaspoon natural sugar

1/2 teaspoon red pepper flakes, or to taste

1 tablespoon minced cilantro leaves

SPRING ROLLS:

8 rice paper wrappers

8 Boston lettuce leaves or other soft leaf lettuce

1 1/2 cups shredded carrot

1 cup fresh bean sprouts

1 ripe avocado, peeled, pitted and cut into strips

1/2 cup chopped cilantro

Spring roll wrappers, made of fragile rice paper, are brittle when you buy them, but soften easily when soaked in water. They are available in Asian markets. Strips of baked tofu make a good addition to these spring rolls. To make this soy-free, use coconut aminos in place of the tamari.

SAUCE: In a small bowl or food processor, combine the peanut butter, tamari, water, vinegar, lime juice, garlic, sugar, and red pepper flakes until well blended. Taste to adjust the seasonings. Add more water if the sauce is too thick. Set aside while you make the spring rolls, or cover and refrigerate until ready to use. Add minced cilantro to the sauce just prior to serving time.

SPRING ROLLS: Dip a wrapper into a shallow bowl of warm water just long enough to soften. Remove the wrapper from the water and place on a piece of plastic wrap on a flat work surface. Place a lettuce leaf on top of the wrapper and arrange a small amount of the carrots, sprouts, avocado, and chopped cilantro on the bottom third of the lettuce leaf. Bring the bottom edge of the wrapper over the filling and fold in the sides tightly. Use your finger to spread water along the top edge and roll tightly, using the plastic wrap to help roll it up.

Place the roll seam side down on a serving platter. Repeat with the remaining wrappers, lettuce, and filling ingredients. When assembly is finished, serve the rolls with the peanut sauce for dipping.

Spice-Rubbed Vegetable Skewers with Cashew Sauce

These tasty skewered vegetables are a crowd pleaser whether plated individually or heaped on a platter and served on a buffet. Be sure to soak the bamboo skewers in cold water for 30 minutes to prevent them from burning. Use coconut aminos instead of tamari to make this soy-free.

In a bowl or food processor, combine the coconut milk, cashew butter, ginger, garlic, sugar, tamari, and lemon juice. Blend until smooth. Transfer to a saucepan and simmer on low heat until slightly thickened, stirring frequently, about 10 minutes. Set aside.

In a small bowl, combine the coriander, cumin, sugar, salt, and cayenne. Set aside.

Preheat the broiler or grill. Place the eggplant, bell pepper, and mushroom in a large bowl and drizzle with the oil. Toss to coat. Sprinkle the vegetables with the reserved spice mixture, tossing to coat. Press any remaining spice mixture from the bottom of the bowl into the vegetables so the spices adhere.

Thread the vegetables onto the skewers and place them under the broiler or on the grill until well browned, 5 to 7 minutes per side.

Arrange the skewered vegetables on plates lined with lettuce leaves. Drizzle the skewers with some of the sauce. Divide the reserved sauce among 4 small dipping bowls, and place them on the plates with the skewered vegetables. Serve at once.

Gluten Free
Soy-Free Option

Serves 4

3/4 cup unsweetened coconut milk

2 tablespoons cashew butter (page 7)

1 tablespoon minced fresh ginger

1 clove garlic, minced

1 tablespoon natural sugar

1 tablespoon wheat-free tamari

1 tablespoon fresh lemon juice

1/2 teaspoon ground coriander

1/2 teaspoon ground cumin

1/4 teaspoon natural sugar

1/4 teaspoon salt

1/4 teaspoon cayenne

2 Japanese eggplants, halved or quartered lengthwise and cut into 1/2-inch slices

1 large red bell pepper, halved lengthwise, seeded, and cut into 1-inch pieces

2 portobello mushroom caps, cut into 1-inch chunks

2 tablespoons toasted sesame oil

4 leaves leaf lettuce

Savory Three-Nut Pâté

Gluten-Free Option
Soy Free

Serves 12

1 tablespoon olive oil or 1/4 cup
    water
1 large yellow onion, minced
2 cloves garlic, minced
1/2 cup almond butter (page 7)
1/4 cup peanut butter (page 7)
1 1/2 tablespoons brandy or water
1 teaspoon wheat-free tamari
3/4 teaspoon dried thyme
1/2 teaspoon salt
1/8 teaspoon cayenne
1 1/2 cups walnut pieces
1 cup cooked lentils or beans (any
    kind), well drained and blotted dry
2 tablespoons chopped fresh parsley
2 tablespoons all-purpose flour

This lovely pâté can be garnished with ground nuts and fresh herbs. It can be served whole or sliced on a buffet table with an assortment of crackers and breads, or serve it warm as a delicious dinner entrée. It also makes a great cold snack right out of the fridge. To make this gluten-free, use a gluten-free flour.

Lightly oil a 6-cup loaf pan or pâté mold. Preheat the oven to 350°F.

Heat the oil or water in a large skillet over medium heat. Add the onion and garlic. Cover and cook until softened. about 5 minutes. Add the almond butter, peanut butter, brandy or water, tamari, thyme, salt, and cayenne, and stir thoroughly blended. Set aside.

Place the walnuts and lentils in a food processor and process until finely chopped. Add the parsley and flour, and pulse to combine. Add the reserved almond butter mixture, and process until well combined. Taste to adjust the seasonings, then spoon the mixture into the prepared pan. Bake until firm, about 45 minutes.

Let the pâté cool at room temperature, then refrigerate it until chilled completely for easier slicing.

When ready to serve, remove the pâté from the mold, or run a knife along the edge of the loaf pan and invert onto a plate.

Fire Ants on a Log

This is a grown-up version of that kindergarten favorite, with a spicy heat that is suited to adult tastes. This recipe can be adjusted to make a solo snack or enough to feed a crowd. If the red color of the cranberries provides enough "fire" for you, you can eliminate the spicy-hot "fire" of the cayenne.

Trim the ends from the celery and, using a vegetable peeler or sharp paring knife, remove a thin strip lengthwise from along the curved back of each celery rib so they sit flat without wobbling. Set aside.

In a bowl, combine the almond butter, maple syrup, and cayenne, stirring to blend.

Stuff the almond butter mixture into the celery pieces and gently press the cranberries into the almond butter.

To serve as a finger food, cut the celery into bite-size pieces (about 1 inch long) and arrange on a platter. Otherwise, they may be cut in half or left whole.

Gluten Free
Soy Free

Serves 4

5 or 6 celery ribs
1/2 cup almond butter (page 7)
1 teaspoon maple syrup
1/4 teaspoon cayenne
1/2 cup sweetened dried cranberries

Belgian Endive with Pineapple-Macadamia Cream Cheese

Gluten Free

Makes about 24

1 (8-ounce) can crushed pineapple, well drained and blotted
8 ounces vegan cream cheese,
  softened
1/3 cup macadamia butter (page 7)
2 heads Belgian endive
1/2 cup coarsely ground toasted
  macadamia nuts
Curly endive (chicory)

This yummy appetizer tastes like dessert and looks especially appealing on a tray when the leaves are arranged to resemble a flower.

In a medium-size bowl, combine the pineapple, cream cheese, and macadamia butter. Blend well and set aside.

Trim the stem end off the endive and separate the individual leaves.

Use a pastry bag, a zip-top bag, or a spoon to distribute about 2 teaspoons of the filling mixture into the bottom of each leaf. Sprinkle the filling with the ground macadamias.

Arrange the filled leaves on a round plate to resemble flower petals, with some curly endive leaves placed in the center of the plate for garnish.

Wonton Crisps with Thai Peanut Spread

Look for vegan wonton wrappers in the refrigerated case of Asian supermarkets (read the ingredients on the label to be sure they don't contain egg). If unavailable, use thin slices of toasted French bread. Use two or more of the topping suggestions on each crisp for a taste and textural contrast. For example, try the shredded cucumber and carrots with chopped peanuts or toasted coconut. Use coconut aminos instead of tamari to make this soy-free.

Preheat the oven to 350°F. Cut the wonton wrapper diagonally to make 24 triangles. Lightly brush both sides of the wrappers with a small amount of neutral vegetable oil. Arrange on baking sheets and bake until crisp, 5 to 7 minutes. Remove from the oven and set aside to cool.

In a bowl, combine the peanut butter, coconut milk, lime juice, tamari, sugar, and red pepper flakes until well blended.

Spread a thin coating of the peanut mixture on each wonton, sprinkle on a small amount of the desired toppings, and serve at once.

Soy-Free Option

Serves 4

12 vegan wonton wrappers (or thin slices of a baguette)
Neutral vegetable oil
1/2 cup peanut butter (page 7)
1/3 cup unsweetened coconut milk
2 tablespoons fresh lime juice
2 teaspoons wheat-free tamari
1 teaspoon natural sugar
1/2 teaspoon red pepper flakes, or to taste
Toppings: shredded green papaya, toasted coconut, shredded cucumber, shredded carrot, chopped roasted peanuts, minced crystallized ginger

Spinach-Walnut Crostini

Gluten Free
Soy Free

Serves 6

3 garlic cloves
Olive oil
9 ounces fresh baby spinach,
  chopped
2 tablespoons walnut butter (page 7)
1/2 teaspoon red pepper flakes
Salt
1 baguette, cut into 1/2-inch-thick
  slices
2 tablespoons chopped toasted
  walnuts

This popular Italian appetizer is made with toasted bread rounds that are usually rubbed with a cut clove of garlic and crowned with a savory topping.

Finely mince two of the garlic cloves and set aside. Cut the remaining garlic clove in half and set aside.

Heat 1 tablespoon olive oil or 1/4 cup of water in a medium skillet over medium heat. Add the minced garlic and cook until fragrant, about 30 seconds. Add the spinach, stirring to wilt. Stir in the walnut butter, red pepper flakes, and salt to taste, blending the walnut butter into the spinach, stirring until any remaining water is absorbed. Keep warm.

Preheat the oven to 400°F. Brush one side of each slice of bread lightly with olive oil. Place the bread, oiled side up, on a baking sheet and bake until golden brown, about 10 minutes. When the bread is toasted, remove it from the oven and rub the oiled side with the cut sides of the halved garlic clove.

Top each piece of bread with a small amount of the spinach topping. Sprinkle with chopped walnuts and serve hot.

Almond Butter and Orange Marmalade Pinwheels

Brimming with color, texture, and flavor, this no-cook appetizer is easy to assemble on a moment's notice.

In a small bowl, combine the almond butter, mayonnaise, celery, and olives. Mix well and set aside.

In a separate bowl, combine the marmalade and grated carrot. Set aside.

Place one piece of the lavash on a cutting board and spread evenly with half of the almond butter mixture. Spread half of the marmalade mixture on top.

Roll up the bread and use a serrated knife to cut the roll into 1-inch pieces. Stand the pieces upright on a platter and repeat with the remaining ingredients.

NOTE: Soft white bread with the crusts removed may be used instead of the lavash or tortillas, if desired.

Serves 4

1/2 cup almond butter (page 7)
2 tablespoons vegan mayonnaise
1/4 cup finely minced celery
2 tablespoons finely minced pitted black olives
1/2 cup orange marmalade
1 large carrot, grated
2 pieces lavash flatbread or flour tortillas

ALMOND BUTTER

Mild in flavor, almond butter is ideal for both sweet and savory dishes. When the almonds start to come away from the sides of the food processor, the butter is ready.

4 Salads

Cold Noodle Salad with Spicy Peanut Sauce

Serves 6

1/2 cup peanut butter (page 7)
4 teaspoons wheat-free tamari
2 tablespoons rice vinegar
1/4 teaspoon cayenne, or to taste
2 cloves garlic, minced
1 teaspoon grated fresh ginger
1/2 cup water
8 ounces linguine or rice noodles
1 tablespoon toasted sesame oil
1 large carrot, shredded
1 red bell pepper, cut into match-
  stick julienne strips
3 scallions, thinly sliced
1/4 cup roasted peanuts or
  cashews

The hint of sesame oil complements the flavor of the peanut butter in this satisfying salad that makes a great make-ahead meal. Linguine noodles are used because they are sturdy and easy to find, but if you prefer, substitute Asian noodles. If you want to bulk up the protein, add 8 ounces of baked diced tofu. To make this gluten-free, use rice noodles or other gluten-free noodles. For soy-free, replace the tamari with coconut aminos.

In a medium bowl, combine the peanut butter, tamari, vinegar, cayenne, garlic, and ginger, stirring to blend well. Add the water (up to 1/2 cup) to make a thick sauce. Set aside.

Cook the noodles in a large pot of boiling water according to package directions. Drain and rinse under cold water and transfer to a large bowl. Toss with the sesame oil to coat.

Add the carrot, bell pepper, and scallions to the bowl with the noodles. Add the reserved peanut sauce to coat, tossing gently to combine. Refrigerate for 30 minutes before serving. Garnish with peanuts just before serving.

Roasted Niçoise Salad with Cashew Goddess Dressing

Roasting the potatoes and green beans adds a new layer of flavor to this hearty salad. A creamy cashew dressing provides a rich finish. To make this soy free, use coconut aminos instead of tamari.

Preheat the oven to 425°F. Arrange the potatoes on a lightly oiled baking pan and spray with a little cooking spray. Season to taste with salt and pepper and roast until just softened and lightly browned, turning once, about 25 minutes. Add the steamed green beans, chickpeas, and tomatoes. Season with salt and pepper, and spray with a little cooking spray. Return to the oven for 15 minutes.

While the vegetables are roasting, make the dressing. Grind the cashews in a high-speed blender. If you don't have a high-speed blender, you can use a food processor but the dressing won't be as smooth. Add the scallions, garlic, and parsley. Pulse to mince. Add the almond milk, tahini, vinegar, lemon juice, tamari, and salt to taste; process until smooth. Set aside.

When the vegetables are roasted, remove from the oven and allow to cool to room temperature.

To serve, arrange the lettuce leaves onto four serving plates. Arrange the vegetables on top and drizzle each salad with some of the dressing. Serve immediately.

Gluten Free
Soy-Free Option

Serves 4

1 pound small new potatoes, halved or cut into 1/2-inch pieces
8 ounces green beans, steamed
1 1/2 cups cooked or 1 (15.5-ounce) can chickpeas, drained and rinsed
1 cup cherry or grape tomatoes, halved lengthwise
1/3 cup cashews
2 scallions, chopped
1 garlic clove, crushed
3 tablespoons chopped fresh parsley
1/2 cup plain unsweetened almond milk
2 tablespoons tahini
2 tablespoons rice vinegar
1 tablespoon fresh lemon juice
1 tablespoon wheat-free tamari
1/2 teaspoon salt
1/3 cup kalamata olives, pitted and halved
Torn butter lettuce leaves, to serve

Mixed Greens and Green Papaya with Thai Peanut Dressing

Gluten Free
Soy-Free Option

Serves 4

2 tablespoons peanut butter (page 7)
1 large clove garlic, finely minced
1 teaspoon minced fresh ginger
1/2 teaspoon red pepper flakes
1 tablespoon natural sugar
1/4 cup fresh lime juice
2 tablespoons wheat-free tamari
1 green papaya, peeled, halved
   lengthwise, and seeded
1 small carrot
4 cups mixed baby greens
1/3 cup chopped roasted peanuts

This refreshing Thai-inspired salad is spicy, sweet, and crunchy. Green papayas are available in Asian markets. The easiest way to shred them is with a mandoline or other slicer, like the Benriner. To make this soy-free, replace the tamari with coconut aminos.

In a small bowl, combine the peanut butter, garlic, ginger, red pepper flakes, and sugar. Blend in the lime juice and tamari, and set aside.

Shred the papaya using a mandoline. If you don't have a mandoline-type slicer, use a box grater, food processor with a shredding disk, or a sharp knife. Place the shredded papaya in a large bowl. Shred the carrot in the same way, place in a separate bowl, and set aside.

Pour about one-third of the reserved dressing over the papaya and toss to combine. Set aside.

Toss the greens with the remaining dressing and arrange on 4 salad plates. Top each salad with a portion of the reserved papaya, and sprinkle each with the chopped peanuts and reserved carrots.

Waldorf Salad with Walnut Butter Dressing

This decidedly nontraditional Waldorf salad features walnut butter and dried cranberries, along with the traditional apples and celery. It makes an especially pretty addition to a holiday dinner table. I like to use sweet Fuji or Gala apples with the peels left on for color and crunch. Be sure to wash the apples really well, especially if they're not organic.

Cut the apples into 1/2-inch dice and place them in a large bowl. Add the lemon juice and toss to coat. Add the celery, half of the walnuts, grapes, cranberries, and scallion (if using), and set aside.

In a small bowl, combine the mayonnaise, walnut butter, sugar, and salt, stirring to blend. Add the sauce to the apple mixture and stir gently to combine. Taste to adjust the seasonings.

Sprinkle with the remaining walnuts and serve at once, or cover and refrigerate until ready to use. This salad is best if served on the same day it is made.

Gluten Free

Serves 4

4 red-skinned apples, cored
1 tablespoon fresh lemon juice
1 cup finely minced celery
1/2 cup toasted walnuts pieces
1/2 cup red or green seedless grapes, halved
1/3 cup dried sweetened cranberries
1 scallion, finely minced (optional)
1/3 cup vegan mayonnaise
1/4 cup walnut butter (page 7)
1/4 teaspoon natural sugar
1/4 teaspoon salt

Crunchy Coleslaw with Creamy Cashew Dressing

Serves 4 to 6

4 cups shredded green cabbage
1 large carrot, grated
2 tablespoons minced cilantro or
   parsley
1/4 cup cashew butter (page 7)
1/4 cup vegan mayonnaise
2 tablespoons fresh lemon juice
1 tablespoon white wine vinegar
1 teaspoon natural sugar
Salt and ground black pepper

The addition of cilantro gives this slaw an exotic Southeast Asian flavor, which can be further amplified by replacing the lemon juice with lime juice and adding a dash of red-pepper flakes. For a more mainstream slaw, use the parsley instead of cilantro. Either way, the cashew butter adds a new and flavorful twist to the popular cabbage salad. The sauce may appear a bit thick at first, but it works out fine once you mix it into the slaw. Lea Jacobson tested this recipe and said it was one of the best coleslaws she's ever eaten.

In a large bowl, combine the cabbage, carrot, and cilantro. Set aside.

In a small bowl, combine the cashew butter, mayonnaise, lemon juice, vinegar, sugar, and salt and pepper to taste. Stir until well blended.

Pour the dressing over the vegetables and toss gently to coat. Taste and adjust seasoning. Refrigerate, covered, until ready to serve.

CASHEW MAGIC

Cashews make a smooth butter that is ideal for using in sauces and desserts. When thinned with liquid, cashew butter turns into a cashew cream that can be used to make sauces for pasta, casseroles, desserts, and more.

Tropical Fruit Salad with Macadamia-Rum Dressing

The dried cranberries produce a vibrant color accent to this lush and sophisticated fruit salad – a far cry from the canned stuff we had as kids. The dressing is also delicious without the rum, so omit it, if you prefer.

In a small bowl, combine the macadamia butter, orange juice, lime juice, rum, and sugar, if using, stirring to blend. Set aside.

In a large bowl, combine the pineapple, orange, mango, apple, and bananas. Add the reserved sauce, then sprinkle with the cranberries, macadamias, and mint.

NOTE: If you prefer, serve the fruit salad with the dressing on the side.

Gluten Free
Soy Free

Serves 6

2 tablespoons macadamia butter (page 7)
2 tablespoons fresh orange juice
1 tablespoon fresh lime juice
1 tablespoon dark rum
1/2 teaspoon natural sugar (optional)
2 cups fresh pineapple chunks
1 navel orange, peeled and cut into 1-inch chunks
1 mango, peeled, halved, and cut into 1-inch chunks
1 apple or ripe pear, cored and cut into 1-inch chunks
2 bananas, sliced
1/4 cup dried sweetened cranberries
1/4 cup roasted macadamia nuts, coarsely chopped
1 tablespoon chopped fresh mint

Pecan Lover's Potato Salad

Gluten Free
....

Serves 6

1 1/2 pounds small red-skinned potatoes, halved or quartered
1 small rib celery, minced
2 tablespoons grated onion
1/3 cup roasted pecan halves or
  pieces
1/2 cup vegan mayonnaise
2 to 3 tablespoons pecan butter
  (page 7)
2 tablespoons minced parsley
Salt and ground black pepper

*This hearty salad, with its rich pecan undertones, is also de-
licious served warm. For a lovely color accent, stir in some
thawed frozen green peas.*

Steam the potatoes over boiling water, until tender but still
firm, 15 to 20 minutes. Drain and place in a large bowl.
Add the celery, onion, and pecans, and set aside.

In a small bowl, combine the mayonnaise, pecan butter,
parsley, and salt and pepper to taste. Mix well and add to
the potato mixture, stirring gently to combine. Serve right
away, or cover and refrigerate until ready to serve.

BUY PIECES, NOT HALVES
....

To save money when shopping for pecans or walnuts for nut butter, buy "pieces," not "halves" – they
are less expensive.

Indonesian Gado-Gado

Gado-Gado is an Indonesian main-dish salad composed of raw and cooked vegetables tossed with a spicy peanut sauce. The flavor improves with time, so plan on making this crunchy salad the day before you need it. To make this soy-free, replace the tamari with coconut aminos.

Heat the oil or water in a skillet over medium heat. Add the shallots and garlic. Cover and cook until softened, about 5 minutes. Stir in the peanut butter, tamari, lemon juice, sugar, cayenne, and coconut milk. Simmer over low heat for 2 minutes, stirring to blend.

Transfer the mixture to a blender or food processor, or use an immersion blender, and puree until smooth, adding water or more coconut milk to thin, if needed.

Steam the green beans and cauliflower just until tender and place them in a large bowl. Add the carrots and cabbage. Pour the sauce over the vegetables and toss to combine. Sprinkle the bean sprouts and peanuts on top. Cover and refrigerate until ready to serve.

Gluten Free
Soy-Free Option

Serves 6

1 tablespoon neutral vegetable oil
  or 1/4 cup water
2 shallots, chopped
1 large clove garlic, chopped
1/2 cup peanut butter (page 7)
1 1/2 tablespoons wheat-free
  tamari
1 1/2 tablespoons fresh lemon
  juice
1 teaspoon natural sugar
1/4 teaspoon cayenne
3/4 cup unsweetened coconut milk
2 cups green beans, cut into 1-inch
  lengths
1 cup small cauliflower florets
2 carrots, shredded
2 cups shredded cabbage
1 cup fresh bean sprouts
1/3 cup roasted peanuts

Roasted Sweet Potato Salad with Almond Butter

Serves 4

1 1/2 pounds sweet potatoes
1 tablespoon olive oil
1 cup frozen baby peas, thawed
2 scallions, minced
1/2 cup pineapple or orange juice
1/4 cup almond butter (page 7)
Salt and ground black pepper
2 tablespoons toasted slivered
  almonds

This colorful dish is both a nice change from regular potato salad and an unusual way to serve sweet potatoes. Almond butter provides a creamy richness to the dressing and toasted almonds add crunch.

Preheat the oven to 400°F. Peel the potatoes and cut them into 1/2-inch dice. Toss with the olive oil and spread on a baking sheet. Roast the potatoes until tender but still firm, about 30 minutes. Allow to cool, then place in a large bowl. Add the peas and scallions, and set aside.

In a small bowl, combine the juice, almond butter, and salt and pepper to taste. Blend well, then pour the dressing over the potato mixture, stirring gently to combine.

Sprinkle with the almonds and serve right away, or cover and refrigerate until ready to serve.

NUTS IN HISTORY

Almonds were among the earliest cultivated foods, probably before 3000 BC.

5 Side Dishes

Grilled Vegetables with Almond Romesco Sauce

Gluten Free
Soy Free

Serves 4

3 large red bell peppers, quartered lengthwise and seeded
1 tablespoon olive oil, plus more for grilling
1 small red chile, seeded and minced
2 tablespoons chopped onion
1 tablespoon chopped garlic
1 (14.5-ounce) can diced tomatoes, drained
2 tablespoons red wine vinegar
1/4 cup almond butter (page 7)
Salt and ground black pepper
3 small zucchini, trimmed and halved lengthwise
4 small Portobello mushrooms, stemmed

This version of Romesco sauce uses a fraction of the olive oil that's in the traditional Spanish sauce. If you don't have a grill, you can broil or sauté the vegetables, with delicious results.

Chop 1 bell pepper and set aside the other 2 peppers.

Heat the 1 tablespoon of oil in a large skillet over medium heat. Add the chopped bell pepper, chile, onion, and garlic, and cook, covered, for 15 minutes. Stir in the tomatoes and vinegar, and cook 15 minutes longer.

Transfer the mixture to a food processor or blender, add the almond butter, and salt and pepper to taste. Process until smooth and creamy. Set aside.

Toss the zucchini, portobellos, and the remaining 2 bell peppers with enough olive oil to lightly coat. Season with salt and pepper, and grill until softened and lightly browned, turning once, 5 to 7 minutes per side.

While the vegetables are cooking, gently heat the reserved sauce.

To serve, transfer the vegetables to a serving platter and spoon the sauce on top, or serve the sauce on the side.

Scalloped Cashew Potatoes and Cauliflower

This decidedly new take on scalloped potatoes combines layers of roasted cauliflower with thinly sliced potatoes baked in a creamy sauce enriched with cashews and almond milk. This is gluten-free if you use gluten-free bread crumbs or ground nuts for the topping. For a colorful variation, substitute sliced butternut squash for the cauliflower.

Preheat oven to 425°F. Lightly oil a baking sheet and a 2-quart baking dish or spray them with cooking spray. Set aside the baking dish.

Arrange the cauliflower on the prepared baking sheet and season with salt and pepper. Drizzle with a little olive oil, if desired, and roast until softened, turning once, about 20 minutes. Remove from the oven and set aside to cool.

In a food processor or high-speed blender, combine the cashews and vegetable broth and process to a paste. Add 1 cup of the smaller pieces of the roasted cauliflower along with the almond milk, lemon juice, garlic powder, thyme, and 1/2 teaspoon salt. Process until very smooth. If the sauce is too thick, add a little extra broth or almond milk.

In the prepared baking dish arrange a layer of potato slices, season with salt and pepper and arrange a layer of cauliflower on top. Continue layering with the remaining potatoes and cauliflower, seasoning with salt and pepper as you layer. Pour the sauce over the vegetables. Cover and bake until the potatoes are tender, about 30 minutes. Uncover and top with the panko or ground nuts, and return to the oven to bake uncovered for 10 minutes more to brown the crumbs. Serve hot.

Gluten-Free Option
Soy Free

Serves 4

1 medium head cauliflower, trimmed, cored, and cut into 1/4-inch slices
Salt and black pepper
Olive oil (optional)
1/2 cup raw cashews
1/2 cup vegetable broth
1/2 cup almond milk
2 tablespoons lemon juice
1/2 teaspoon garlic powder
1 teaspoon dried thyme
1 1/2 pounds Russet or Yukon Gold potatoes, peeled and cut into 1/8-inch slices
1/4 cup panko bread crumbs or ground cashews or walnuts

Indonesian Eggplant with Peanut Sauce

Gluten Free
Soy-Free Option

Serves 4

1 large eggplant, trimmed
1 tablespoon olive oil
Salt and ground black pepper
1 cup unsweetened coconut milk
1/4 cup peanut butter (page 7)
1 clove garlic, minced
1 tablespoon natural sugar
1 tablespoon fresh lemon juice
1 tablespoon wheat-free tamari
1/8 teaspoon cayenne, or to taste
1 tablespoon minced fresh parsley

In the classic Indonesian dish, called Petjel Terong, *the eggplant is usually deep-fried. In this healthier version, the eggplant is baked in the oven with a small amount of olive oil. In the words of recipe tester Jonathan Shanes, this dish "looks terrific, smells divine, and tastes wonderful. The creaminess of the coconut milk and the peanut butter are heavenly. As a side dish, this serves 4, but will serve 3 as a main dish. To make this soy-free, use coconut aminos to replace the tamari.*

Preheat the oven to 425°F. Halve the eggplant lengthwise, then cut each half crosswise into 1/4-inch-thick slices. Arrange the eggplant slices on a lightly oiled baking sheet, brush them with the olive oil, and season with salt and pepper to taste. Bake, turning once, until softened and browned on both sides, about 15 minutes.

While the eggplant is baking, make the sauce. In a medium saucepan, combine the coconut milk, peanut butter, garlic, sugar, lemon juice, tamari, and cayenne. Bring to a boil, then reduce the heat to low and simmer, stirring frequently, until the sauce thickens slightly, about 5 minutes.

Arrange the eggplant slices on a platter and top with the sauce. Garnish with the parsley.

Spicy Walnut Green Beans

If you don't want the heat of the red pepper flakes, there's no need to pass on this dish — it's very flavorful without them. Mirin is a sweet Japanese cooking wine made from rice. It is available in supermarkets, Asian markets, and natural food stores. To make this soy-free, use coconut aminos instead of tamari.

Steam the green beans just until tender, about 5 minutes. Rinse under cold water to stop the cooking process. Drain and set aside.

In a small bowl, combine the walnut butter, tamari, sesame oil, mirin, and sugar and set aside.

Heat the oil in a wok or large skillet over medium-high heat. Add the reserved beans in batches and stir-fry for 30 seconds, transferring the cooked beans to a platter.

When all the beans have been removed, add the garlic, ginger, and red pepper flakes to the same pan and stir-fry for 10 seconds.

Return the beans to the pan and stir-fry for 30 seconds.

Add the reserved walnut butter mixture and stir-fry until the beans are hot and coated with the sauce, about 30 seconds.

Gluten Free
Soy-Free Option

Serves 4

1 1/2 pounds green beans, trimmed
2 tablespoons walnut butter (page 7)
2 tablespoons wheat-free tamari
2 teaspoons toasted sesame oil
1 tablespoon mirin or water
1/2 teaspoon sugar
1 tablespoon neutral vegetable oil
1 large clove garlic, minced
1 teaspoon minced fresh ginger
1/2 teaspoon red pepper flakes, or to taste

Braised Carrots with Macadamia Butter

Gluten Free
Soy-Free Option

Serves 4

3 tablespoons wheat-free tamari

1 1/2 tablespoons macadamia butter (page 7)

1 1/2 tablespoons pure maple syrup

1/8 teaspoon cayenne

2/3 cup water

6 large carrots, trimmed and sliced diagonally

2 tablespoons chopped toasted macadamia nuts

The thick flavorful glaze turns everyday carrots into a special treat. To make this soy-free, use coconut aminos instead of tamari.

In a small bowl, whisk together the tamari, macadamia butter, maple syrup, cayenne, and water until smooth. Set aside.

Steam the carrots over boiling water until slightly softened, 4 to 5 minutes. Set aside.

In a large skillet over medium heat, combine the carrots and the reserved soy-macadamia mixture, stirring to combine. Reduce the heat to low. Cover and cook, stirring occasionally, until the carrots are soft and well glazed, about 8 minutes. Serve hot garnished with the macadamia nuts.

Curried Cashew Chicory Fritters

Serve these fritters with applesauce or chutney on the side. If you're not a curry fan, omit the curry powder and add 2 tablespoons chopped roasted cashews. For a spicy version, add some cayenne or minced jalapeño. To make this gluten-free, use a gluten-free flour.

Preheat the oven to 250°F. Blanch the chicory in a pot of boiling salted water. Drain well and place in a large bowl. Add the onion and cashew butter, and mix well.

Stir in the flour, curry powder, salt, and pepper to taste. Mix until well combined.

Heat a thin layer of oil in a large nonstick skillet over medium heat. Scoop a large spoonful of the vegetable mixture and press it with your hand to pack firmly. Repeat until all of the vegetable mixture is used. You should have about 8 small fritters.

Cook the fritters in the hot pan, in batches, until they are golden brown on both sides, about 5 minutes. Add more oil to the pan as necessary.

Drain the cooked fritters on paper towels and transfer to the oven to keep warm until all the fritters are cooked. Serve hot.

NOTE: If you prefer a finer texture, puree the vegetable mixture in a food processor before cooking. Other dark greens such as kale, chard, escarole, or spinach may be used instead of the chicory.

Gluten-Free Option
Soy Free

Serves 4

1 head chicory (curly endive), washed, trimmed, and chopped
1 small yellow onion, grated
2 tablespoons cashew butter (page 7)
1/2 cup all-purpose flour
1 teaspoon curry powder
1 teaspoon salt
ground black pepper
Neutral vegetable oil

Almond Mashed Potato Cakes

Gluten Free
Soy Free

Serves 4

1 3/4 cups cold mashed potatoes
1/4 cup all-purpose flour, plus
   more for dredging
2 tablespoons almond butter (page 7)
2 scallions, minced
1 tablespoon minced fresh parsley
Salt and ground black pepper
2 tablespoons olive oil

Almond butter enriches the flavor of these potato pancakes, made with cold leftover mashed potatoes. The outside becomes crisp and brown, while the inside remains soft. In addition to a great dinner side dish, these cakes also make a terrific breakfast or brunch dish. If you don't have mashed potatoes on hand, you'll need a little over one pound of potatoes to make the 1 3/4 cups mashed needed for this recipe. For crispier cakes, dredge them in panko crumbs instead of flour before frying.

Place the potatoes in a bowl. Add the 1/4 cup flour, almond butter, scallions, parsley, and salt and pepper to taste. Mix well.

Scoop out a spoonful of the potato mixture and, using your hands, shape into a small patty. Repeat until all the mixture is used up. You should have 8 to 10 cakes. Dredge them in the extra flour and set aside.

Heat the oil in a large nonstick skillet over medium-high heat. Add the potato cakes, in batches, and cook until crisp and golden brown on both sides, about 10 minutes.

Cheesy Almond Brocolli Soup, 17

West African Vegetable Stew, 73

Curried Almond Sweet Potato Soup, 15

Asian Spring Rolls with Spicy Peanut Dipping Sauce, 32

Smoke and Spice Almond Hummus, 28

Roasted Niçoise Salad with Cashew Goddess Dressing, 43

Indonesian Gado-Gado, 49

Spicy Walnut Green Beans, 55

Grilled Vegetables with Almond Romesco Sauce, 52

Penne Primavera with Avocado Cashew Cream, 70

Szechuan Stir-Fry with Fiery Peanut Sauce, 78

Peach-Almond Butter Quesadillas, 89

Thai Tofu-Vegetable Wraps, 91

Apple-Almond Butter Pancakes, 99

(clockwise from left) Handcrafted Granola Sunflower Bars, 103; Peanut Butter and Banana Smoothie, 104; Cranberry-Pecan Butter Muffins, 100

Peanut Butter Cups, 127

Grilled Fruit Satays with Pineapple-Coconut Peanut Sauce, 123

Chocolate Macadamia Truffles with Coconut, 129

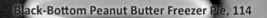
Black-Bottom Peanut Butter Freezer Pie, 114

Mashed Sweet Potato Pecan Bake

Pecan butter and apple juice add their unique flavor notes to this sweet potato casserole enlivened with cinnamon and nutmeg. This can be soy-free if you use a soy-free vegan butter.

Cook the sweet potatoes in a large saucepan of boiling water until tender, 15 to 20 minutes.

While the potatoes are cooking, combine 1 tablespoon of the sugar with the apple juice, pecan butter, butter, cinnamon, nutmeg, and vanilla in a small bowl and blend until smooth. Set aside.

When the sweet potatoes are cooked, drain them well and return them to the saucepan. Add the reserved pecan butter mixture and season with salt and pepper to taste. Mash until smooth and well combined.

Preheat the oven to 400°F. Lightly grease a shallow 1 1/2-quart baking dish. Transfer the sweet potato mixture to the prepared dish and sprinkle with the pecans and the remaining 1 tablespoon sugar. Bake until hot, about 30 minutes.

Gluten Free
Soy-Free Option

Serves 4 to 6

3 large sweet potatoes, peeled and diced
2 tablespoons natural sugar
2 tablespoons apple juice
2 tablespoons pecan butter (page 7)
1 tablespoon vegan butter
1/2 teaspoon ground cinnamon
1/2 teaspoon ground nutmeg
1/2 teaspoon vanilla extract
Salt and ground black pepper
1/4 cup crushed pecan pieces

A PECAN TIP

Pecans make a smooth butter with a rich, hearty flavor. To avoid a slightly bitter taste, it's best to roast the pecans before processing into butter.

Roasted Tahini Cauliflower

Gluten Free
Soy Free

Serves 4

1 head cauliflower, cut into bite-
  sized florets
2 tablespoons olive oil
Salt and black pepper
2 to 3 garlic cloves
1 teaspoon za'atar spice mix
1/2 teaspoon ground cumin
1/2 teaspoon ground coriander
1/2 teaspoon sesame seeds
1/4 teaspoon smoked paprika
1/2 cup tahini (sesame butter)
  (page 8)
Juice of 1 large lemon
1/4 teaspoon sriracha or other hot
  sauce
1/4 cup water
Lemon wedges, to serve

This roasted cauliflower dish from the Middle East is known as zahra mekhla. *It calls for coating the cauliflower in a flavorful tahini sauce.*

Preheat oven to 450°F. Toss cauliflower in 1 tablespoon of the olive oil. Season with salt and pepper, and spread in a single layer on a baking pan. Bake until nicely browned and tender, about 25 minutes, turning once about halfway through.

While the cauliflower is roasting, heat the remaining 1 tablespoon of oil in a small skillet. Add the garlic and sauté until softened and fragrant, about 1 minute. Stir in the za'atar spices, cumin, coriander, sesame seeds, and paprika, then stir in the tahini, lemon juice, and sriracha. Season with salt and pepper and stir in the water, stirring until smooth. Taste and adjust the seasonings, if needed.

To serve, toss the hot roasted cauliflower in the sauce and serve immediately.

ALLERGY ALERT

If you are allergic to peanuts (or another nut), determine through a medical practitioner if you are also allergic to other nuts. You may be able to tolerate another type of nut butter or sunflower seed butter or soy nut butter, and you can use them to make any of the recipes in this book.

Spinach with Sesame Sauce

Combining spinach with a creamy sauce is a universally popular way to enjoy these iron-rich greens. This Japanese side dish of cooked spinach coated with a ground sesame seed sauce is called gomai. It is typically served at room temperature, but is also delicious served hot. For a different flavor twist, use peanut butter or almond butter instead of sesame butter.

In a small bowl, combine the coconut milk and sesame butter until blended. Set aside.

Heat the oil or water in a large skillet over medium heat. Add the ginger and cumin, and cook for 30 seconds. Add the spinach and stir-fry until wilted, about 2 minutes.

Stir in the reserved sesame butter mixture, and salt and pepper to taste. Simmer, stirring frequently, until creamy, 5 to 7 minutes.

Serve hot or at room temperature, sprinkled with gomasio, if using.

Gluten Free
Soy Free

Serves 4

3/4 cup unsweetened coconut milk
3 tablespoons sesame butter (page 8)
1 tablespoon neutral vegetable oil
   or 1/4 cup water
1 teaspoon grated fresh ginger
1/2 teaspoon ground cumin
1 pound fresh baby spinach, well
   washed
Salt and ground black pepper
Gomasio, optional garnish

6 Main Dishes

Almond-Quinoa Fireballs

Serves 4

ALMOND-QUINOA BALLS:
3/4 cup cooked quinoa
1/2 cup old-fashioned rolled oats
1/4 cup almond butter (page 7)
1 teaspoon salt
1/2 teaspoon black pepper
1 1/2 cups cooked or 1
   (15.5-ounce) can white beans,
   well drained and blotted dry
Olive oil or cooking spray

FIRE SAUCE:
2 tablespoons almond butter (page 7)
2 tablespoons Asian sweet chili
   sauce
2 tablespoons sriracha sauce
1 tablespoon vegan mayonnaise

Instead of baking these flavorful and nutritious bites, you can fry them in a skillet in a little oil. They can be enjoyed as a main dish, an appetizer, or in a sandwich. Use gluten-free oats to make this gluten-free.

ALMOND-QUINOA BALLS: Preheat the oven to 350°F. Lightly oil a baking sheet or spray it with cooking spray and set aside.

In a food processor, combine the cooked quinoa, oats, almond butter, and salt and pepper and process until well mixed. Add the white beans and pulse until you have a stiff mixture. Roll into 1 1/2-inch balls and arrange on the prepared baking sheet. Bake for 30 minutes or until golden brown.

FIRE SAUCE : Combine all the sauce ingredients in a bowl or blender and stir or process to blend thoroughly.

To serve: Either combine the balls and fire sauce in a bowl and toss gently to coat, or transfer the balls to a shallow bowl and drizzle the sauce on top.

Vegetable-Cashew Korma

Rich and decadent, this flavorful dish is loaded with vegetables. You can substitute cauliflower for the broccoli or add steamed green beans in place of the peas. Serve alone with warm naan or other flatbread, or serve over fragrant cooked basmati rice.

Drain the cashews and transfer them to a high-speed blender or food processor. Add 1 cup of the broth and process until very smooth. Set aside.

Steam the potatoes and broccoli over boiling water, either separately or together, depending on the size of your steamer, until just tender but not soft, 10 to 15 minutes. If steaming the vegetables together, start with the potatoes, then about 7 minutes later add the broccoli, in order for them to be done around the same time. Remove from the heat, uncover, and set aside.

In a food processor, combine the onion, garlic, jalapeños, and ginger and puree until smooth.

Heat the oil in a large pot over medium heat. Add the pureed onion mixture and salt to taste. Cook, stirring, for 10 minutes to cook off any raw taste. Do not burn. Stir in the coriander, garam masala, and salt and pepper to taste. Cook, stirring, for 2 minutes. Add the tomatoes and their juice, chickpeas, and remaining 1 1/2 cups of vegetable broth and bring to a boil. Reduce heat to a simmer and stir in the reserved cashew cream and the coconut milk. Cook uncovered over low heat for about 15 minutes, until slightly thickened. Stir in the spinach, peas, cilantro, and reserved steamed vegetables, and heat until hot. Add the lime juice, then taste and adjust the seasonings if needed. Serve hot.

Gluten Free
Soy Free

Serves 6

1 cup raw cashew pieces, soaked in water for 3 hours or overnight

2 1/2 cups vegetable broth, divided

1 pound Yukon gold potatoes, cut into 1-inch dice

3 cups small broccoli or cauliflower florets

1 large sweet yellow onion

4 cloves garlic

2 jalapeños, seeded and minced

2 teaspoons grated fresh ginger

1 tablespoon neutral vegetable oil

1 tablespoon ground coriander

1 tablespoon garam masala

Salt and black pepper

1 (14.5-ounce) can petite diced tomatoes, undrained

1 1//2 cups cooked or 1 (15.5-ounce) can chickpeas, drained and rinsed

1 cup coconut milk

8 ounces fresh baby spinach

1 cup frozen green peas, thawed

1/2 cup chopped fresh cilantro

1 tablespoon lime juice

Pasta with Cauliflower-Cashew Alfredo

Gluten-Free Option
Soy Free

Serves 4 to 6

1 head cauliflower, cored and cut into 1-inch pieces
1 pound pasta of choice
1 cup raw cashews, soaked overnight
1 cup hot vegetable broth
Salt
1/4 cup plain unsweetened almond milk
4 scallions, chopped
3 tablespoons nutritional yeast
1/4 cup white wine
3 tablespoons fresh lemon juice
1/2 teaspoon garlic powder
1/8 teaspoon cayenne pepper
1 cup cherry or grape tomatoes, halved lengthwise
2 tablespoons pitted kalamata olives, halved
2 tablespoons fresh minced parsley, basil, or chives

This Alfredo sauce blends cashews and cooked cauliflower for a creamy sauce that only tastes indulgent. I like to add sweet grape tomatoes, salty olives, and a fresh herb for extra color, texture, and flavor. If olives aren't your thing, leave them out. You can also include more veggies if you like such as cooked broccoli florets or asparagus, or thawed frozen green peas (added when you add the tomatoes). To make this gluten-free, use gluten-free pasta.

Steam the cauliflower until just tender. Remove from the heat, uncover, and set aside.

Cook the pasta in a pot of boiling salted water until just tender. Drain well and return to the pot.

While the pasta is cooking, drain the soaked cashews and transfer to a high-speed blender or food processor. Add the 1 cup of hot broth, and process until smooth and creamy. Add 2 cups of the steamed cauliflower, almond milk, scallions, nutritional yeast, wine, lemon juice, garlic powder, cayenne, 1/2 teaspoon salt, and blend until very smooth. Taste and adjust the seasonings if needed.

For a thicker sauce, add more cauliflower. For a thinner sauce, add more almond milk. Add the sauce to the cooked, drained pasta.

Add the tomatoes, any remaining cauliflower, and the olives, and toss gently to combine. Serve hot sprinkled with parsley.

Noodles and Greens with Gingery Almond Sauce

In this satisfying peanut-free alternative to traditional peanut sauce, the ginger, garlic, and sesame blend to create a robust flavor combination that will have everyone in your family (including kids!) clamoring for more. This recipe is from my friend Allison Rivers Samson, founder of award-winning AllisonsGourmet.com, the premiere vegan bakery, confectionary & chocolaterie. Allison also writes the acclaimed column "Veganize It!" for VegNews Magazine. Allison likes to use brown rice spaghetti in this dish, but it can be made with whatever noodles or pasta you prefer.

Cook the noodles in a pot of boiling salted water according to package directions. Drain well and return to the pot. Add 1 tablespoon of the sesame oil and toss to combine. Set aside.

In a large skillet over medium-high heat, add the remaining 1 tablespoon sesame oil, sesame seeds, and greens. Sauté for 5 minutes, or until the greens are bright in color and wilted.

In a small saucepan, whisk together the remaining ingredients. Cook over low heat, whisking as it bubbles gently. Cook for 5 to 8 minutes. Cook longer for a thicker sauce, or add water for a thinner sauce.

To serve, place a mound of greens on a bed of noodles, and drizzle the sauce over the top.

Gluten Free

....

Serves 6

12 ounces whole-grain gluten-free spaghetti or rice noodles

2 tablespoons toasted sesame oil

1 tablespoon sesame seeds

2 large bunches kale or chard, washed well and chopped finely

1 cup water

1/2 cup roasted almond butter (page 7)

1/4 cup wheat-free tamari

2 tablespoons brown rice vinegar

1 tablespoon mirin

2 teaspoons freshly grated ginger

1 teaspoon minced garlic

Quinoa and Black Beans with Cashew Queso Sauce

Gluten Free
Soy Free

Serves 4

1 1/2 cup quinoa, well rinsed
2 1/4 cup vegetable broth or water
2 cups cooked or 1 (16-ounce) can black beans, rinsed and drained
3 scallions, minced
2 tablespoons sliced pickled jalapeños
1 (14.5-ounce) can petite diced tomatoes, well drained
2 tablespoons minced fresh cilantro
2/3 cup raw cashews, soaked 3 hours or overnight
3/4 cup hot vegetable broth
Salt
3 tablespoons nutritional yeast
1/2 teaspoon garlic powder
1/2 teaspoon onion powder
1/2 teaspoon smoked paprika
1/4 teaspoon prepared yellow mustard
1/4 teaspoon black pepper
1 tablespoon fresh lemon juice

Hearty quinoa and black beans are topped with a zesty queso sauce in this satisfying dish. Serve with a salad, or sautéed or roasted green vegetable, or add some cooked vegetables such as broccoli florets, on top of the quinoa mixture. When ready to serve, top with the sauce. You might want to make a double batch of the flavorful sauce to use as a dip for chips or to top roasted vegetables.

Combine the quinoa and broth in a saucepan and bring to a boil. Reduce the heat to a simmer, add salt to taste, cover, and cook for 25 minutes. Stir in the beans and scallions, and cook until the quinoa is tender, about 5 minutes longer. Taste and adjust the seasonings, if needed. Stir in the jalapeños, tomatoes, and cilantro and remove from the heat. Set aside covered to keep warm.

While the quinoa is cooking, make the sauce. Drain the cashews and transfer to a high-speed blender or food processor. Add the hot broth and process until smooth and creamy. Add the remaining ingredients and process until very smooth. Taste and adjust the seasonings if needed.

To serve, divide the quinoa mixture among shallow bowls and top each serving with some of the sauce.

Soba and Edamame with Sesame Butter Sauce

This delectable recipe is a one-dish feast made with buckwheat soba and protein-rich edamame. Instead of spinach, you can substitute 1 to 2 cups of a cooked vegetable such as broccoli florets, sliced carrots, or cauliflower. The nutritious sauce made with cannellini beans and sesame butter, cloaks the noodles and vegetables with creamy goodness.

Cook the soba noodles in a large pot of boiling water. When the water begins to boil, pour a cup of cold water into the pot. Bring it to a boil again, pour in another cup of cold water. Repeat 4 or 5 times. This will keep the water from boiling over and helps the noodles cook perfectly. After about 2 minutes of cooking, add the edamame to the noodles. Just before draining, stir in the spinach to wilt. Drain the cooked noodles and vegetables, rinse with cold water, drain again, and return to the pot. Add the sesame oil. Toss to combine.

While the noodles are cooking, heat the vegetable oil or water in a saucepan over medium heat. Add the onion and cook, stirring occasionally, until softened, about 5 minutes. Add the garlic and cook for 1 minute. Add the beans, sesame butter, soy sauce, lemon juice, and salt and pepper to taste, and stir to blend the flavors. Transfer the mixture to a food processor or blender. Add the hot broth and half of the scallions. Puree until smooth and creamy.

Add the sauce to the pot containing the drained cooked noodles and vegetables. Toss gently to combine. Serve at room temperature sprinkled with the remaining scallions and sesame seeds, if using.

Serves 4

8 to 10 ounces soba noodles
1 1/2 cups fresh or frozen shelled edamame
8 ounces fresh baby spinach
2 teaspoons toasted sesame oil
1 tablespoon neutral vegetable oil or 1/4 cup water
1 small yellow onion, chopped
3 garlic cloves, chopped
1 cup cooked cannellini beans, rinsed and drained
1/4 cup sesame butter (page 8) or almond butter (page 7)
1 tablespoon wheat-free tamari
1 tablespoon lemon juice
Salt and ground black pepper
1 cup hot vegetable broth or water, or more if needed
2 tablespoons finely minced scallions
2 teaspoons black sesame seeds (optional)

Penne Primavera with Avocado Cashew Cream

Gluten-Free Option
Soy Free

Serves 4

12 to 16 ounces penne pasta
1 1/2 cups small broccoli florets
1 small carrot, thinly sliced
1 small zucchini or yellow squash, cut into 1/4-inch dice
1/2 cup raw cashews, soaked overnight and drained
1 to 2 garlic cloves, crushed
1 cup hot vegetable broth or water, or more if needed
1 to 2 ripe Hass avocados, halved and pitted
2 scallions, chopped
2 tablespoons lemon juice
1/2 teaspoon salt
ground black pepper
Plain unsweetened almond milk, if needed
1 cup grape tomatoes, halved lengthwise
1/3 cup chopped fresh basil leaves or parsley
Whole fresh basil leaves, for garnish

I like to use penne pasta in this recipe, but any bite-sized pasta will work well. This dish is best if eaten immediately after prepared since the sauce may begin to turn brown if made in advance. Use gluten-free pasta to make this gluten-free.

Cook the penne in a large pot of salted boiling water, stirring occasionally, until it is tender, about 10 minutes. About 5 minutes before the pasta is cooked, add the broccoli and carrots. About 2 minutes before the pasta is cooked, add the zucchini. Drain the cooked pasta and vegetables well and return to the pot.

While the pasta is cooking, combine the drained cashews, garlic, and broth in a high-speed blender or food processor. Process until smooth and well blended. Peel and pit the avocado and add it to the food processor along with the scallions, lemon juice, salt, and pepper to taste. Process until smooth and creamy. For a thinner sauce, add some almond milk, if needed. For a thicker sauce, add additional avocado. Taste and adjust the seasonings, if needed.

Add the sauce to the pot containing the drained cooked pasta and vegetables. Add the tomatoes and chopped basil and toss gently to combine. Serve immediately, garnished with the whole basil leaves.

Sweet Potato and Red Bean Stew

This colorful stew combines almond butter with sweet pota-toes and dark red kidney beans for a hearty dish that is both nourishing and delicious.

Heat the oil or water in a large pot over medium heat. Add the onion and cook, covered, until softened, about 5 minutes.

Add the bell pepper and garlic. Cover and cook until softened, about 5 minutes.

Stir in the sugar, ginger, cumin, and cayenne and cook for 30 seconds. Add the sweet potato and stir to coat with the spices.

Stir in the tomatoes and broth, and season with salt to taste. Bring to a boil, then reduce the heat to low, add the kidney beans, and simmer until the vegetables are soft, about 30 minutes.

In a small bowl, combine the almond butter and 1 cup or more of the liquid from the stew, stirring until blended, then stir it into the stew. Taste to adjust seasonings. Serve hot, sprinkled with chopped almonds.

Gluten Free
Soy Free

Serves 4

1 tablespoon olive oil or 1/4 cup water
1 large yellow onion, chopped
1 large red bell pepper, chopped
1 large clove garlic, minced
1 teaspoon natural sugar
1 teaspoon grated fresh ginger
1/2 teaspoon ground cumin
1/4 teaspoon ground cayenne
1 large sweet potato, peeled and cut into 1/2-inch chunks
1 (14.5-ounce) can diced fire-roasted tomatoes, drained
2 cups vegetable broth
Salt
1 1/2 cups cooked dark red kidney beans or 1 (15.5-ounce) can, drained and rinsed
1/3 cup almond butter (page 7)
1/4 cup chopped roasted almonds

Tropical Chickpea-Brazil Nut Stew

Serves 6

1 tablespoon olive oil or 1/4 cup water

1 large yellow onion, diced

1 large carrot, halved lengthwise and cut into 1/4-inch slices

1 large sweet potato, peeled and cut into 1/2-inch dice

4 ounces green beans, cut into 1-inch pieces

2 cloves garlic, minced

1 fresh hot or mild chile, seeded and minced

1 tablespoon curry powder, or to taste

1 teaspoon natural sugar

3 cups cooked or 2 (15.5-ounce) cans chickpeas, drained and rinsed

2 cups vegetable broth or water

1 (14.5-ounce) can diced tomatoes, undrained

Salt and ground black pepper

1/2 cup Brazil nut butter (page 7)

1 cup frozen peas, thawed

1/4 cup chopped roasted Brazil nuts

1/4 cup chopped pineapple (optional)

For a thicker consistency, scoop out a cup or so of the stew and puree it in a blender or food processor, then stir it back into the pot – or use an immersion blender right in the pot. Serve over brown basmati rice. Variations can include using broccoli or cauliflower in place of the carrot or green beans. Almond butter or cashew butter are delicious alternatives to the Brazil nut butter.

Heat the oil or water in a large saucepan over medium heat. Add the onion and carrot and cook, covered, until softened, about 5 minutes. Stir in the sweet potato, green beans, garlic, chile, curry powder, and sugar, and cook for 1 minute, stirring to coat the vegetables with the spices. Add the chickpeas, broth, tomatoes, and salt and pepper to taste. Bring to a boil, then reduce the heat to low.

Place the Brazil nut butter in a small bowl and add about 1 cup of the cooking liquid, stirring until smooth. Mix into the stew, then cover and simmer until the vegetables are soft, about 30 minutes.

About 10 minutes before the end of the cooking time, remove the lid and add the peas. Simmer uncovered.

Serve sprinkled with chopped Brazil nuts and pineapple, if using.

West African Vegetable Stew

Brimming with vegetables, this flavorful stew is especially good served over rice or couscous or with coarse whole grain bread. Like most stews, this one tastes even better the second day, so make it ahead. The crops of peanuts (or groundnuts), sweet potatoes (or yams), and okra can be found throughout western African countries, where stews such as this are often called groundnut stew.

Heat the oil or water in a large saucepan over medium heat. Add the onion, sweet potato, and bell pepper and cook for 5 minutes. Stir in the eggplant, okra, and garlic. Cover and cook 5 minutes longer, then stir in the tomatoes and cook for a few minutes.

In a small bowl, combine the peanut butter and broth, stirring until smooth. Stir the peanut butter mixture into the stew and season with cayenne, salt, and pepper. Simmer until the vegetables are tender, about 30 minutes.

For a thicker consistency, scoop out about 1 cup of the stew and puree it in a blender or food processor, then return it to the pot.

Gluten Free
Soy Free

Serves 4

1 tablespoon neutral vegetable oil or 1/4 cup water
1 large yellow onion, chopped
1 sweet potato, peeled and diced
1 green bell pepper, chopped
1 medium eggplant, diced
1 cup sliced okra (fresh or frozen)
1 clove garlic, minced
1 (14.5-ounce) can diced tomatoes, undrained
1/2 cup peanut butter (page 7)
1 1/2 cups vegetable broth
1/4 teaspoon cayenne, or to taste
1/2 teaspoon salt
1/8 teaspoon ground black pepper

Linguine with Thai Pesto

Gluten-Free Option
Soy Free

Serves 4

2 large cloves garlic
1 Thai bird chile, halved lengthwise and seeded
1 stalk lemongrass, white part only, chopped
1 teaspoon natural sugar
1/2 teaspoon salt
1 cup Thai basil leaves
1/2 cup cilantro leaves
1/2 cup parsley leaves
1/3 cup peanut butter (page 7)
3 tablespoons water
2 tablespoons fresh lime juice
12 ounces linguine
1/2 cup chopped roasted peanuts

Redolent of garlic, lemongrass, and pungent herbs, this Asian-style pesto makes a fabulous fusion dish when combined with linguine. Most of these ingredients, including the slender, hot Thai chile, are available in supermarkets. Thai basil can be found in Asian markets, as can any of the other ingredients that your regular market may not stock. To make this gluten-free, use gluten-free pasta.

Combine the garlic, chile, lemongrass, sugar, and salt in a food processor and process to a paste. Add the basil, cilantro, and parsley and process until finely ground. Add the peanut butter, water, and lime juice and blend thoroughly, scraping down the sides of the bowl as needed. Set aside.

Cook the linguine in a large pot of salted water just until tender, about 12 minutes. Drain, reserving about 1/2 cup of the water. Toss the pasta with the sauce, adding a little of the hot pasta water, if necessary, to thin the sauce. Garnish with peanuts and serve immediately.

Stuffed Squash with Brazil Nuts and Pistachios

Use a dense, sweet, orange-fleshed squash such as buttercup, acorn, or kabocha for the best results. This flavorful and colorful dish makes an attractive entrée for a Thanksgiving dinner. I like to use Brazil nut butter in this recipe, but you can use any type that you prefer.

Preheat the oven to 350°F. Heat the oil or water in a large skillet over medium heat. Add the onion, cover, and cook until softened, about 5 minutes. Add the garlic and cook until fragrant, about 30 seconds.

Stir in the rice, wild rice, Brazil nut butter, cranberries, nuts, parsley, tarragon, and salt and pepper to taste. Mix well and spoon the mixture into the squash cavities.

Place the squash halves in a baking dish, stuffing sides up. Add the water to the bottom of the baking dish and cover tightly with a lid or aluminum foil. Bake until the squash is tender, about 1 1/2 hours.

Gluten Free
Soy Free

Serves 4

- 1 tablespoon olive oil or 1/4 cup water
- 1 yellow onion, minced
- 2 cloves garlic, minced
- 2 cups cooked brown rice
- 1 cup cooked wild rice
- 1/3 cup Brazil nut butter (page 7)
- 1/4 cup sweetened dried cranberries
- 2 tablespoons chopped pistachio nuts
- 2 tablespoons chopped Brazil nuts
- 1 tablespoon minced fresh parsley
- 1 teaspoon dried tarragon
- Salt and ground black pepper
- 1 large winter squash, halved and seeded (such as buttercup, acorn, or kabocha)
- 1 1/2 cups hot water

NUT? DRUPE? LEGUME?

Not all nuts are nuts. For example, almonds and coconuts are drupes and peanuts are actually legumes.

Chestnut and Winter Vegetable Pot Pie

Gluten-Free Option
Soy-Free Option

Serves 6

This pot pie is comfort food at its finest — thanks, in part, to the chestnut butter, which enriches the creamy sauce. For gluten-free, use gluten-free flour. For soy-free, use coconut aminos in place of the tamari and soy-free vegan butter.

FILLING

1 cup green beans, cut into 1-inch pieces
1 carrot, chopped
1 all-purpose potato, cut into 1/2-inch dice
1 cup vegetable broth
1/4 cup chestnut butter (page 7)
1/2 tablespoon wheat-free tamari
1 tablespoon cornstarch dissolved in 2 tablespoons cold water
1/4 teaspoon dried thyme
1/4 teaspoon dried tarragon (optional)
Salt and ground black pepper
1 tablespoon olive oil or 1/4 cup water
1 yellow onion, chopped
3/4 cup frozen corn kernels, thawed
3/4 cup frozen peas, thawed
1/3 cup chopped roasted chestnuts

CRUST

1 1/4 cups all-purpose flour
1/4 teaspoon salt
1/3 cup vegan butter
3 tablespoons ice water

FILLING: Steam the green beans, carrot, and potato over a pot of boiling water until tender, about 10 minutes. Set aside.

In a small saucepan, blend the broth, chestnut butter, and tamari, and bring to a boil. Reduce the heat to low, and whisk in the cornstarch mixture. Simmer, stirring, until thickened, 2 minutes. Stir in the thyme and tarragon, if using, and season to taste with salt and pepper. Remove from the heat and set aside.

Heat the oil or water in a medium skillet over medium heat. Add the onion, cover, and cook until softened, 5 minutes. Transfer the onion to a 1 1/2- to 2-quart casserole dish. Stir in the corn, peas, chestnuts, green bean mixture, and reserved sauce. Set aside.

CRUST: Preheat the oven to 350°F. In a food processor, combine the flour and salt, pulsing to blend. Add the butter and process until the mixture is crumbly. With the machine running, slowly add the water and process until the mixture forms a ball.

Roll out the dough on a lightly floured surface until it is slightly larger than the rim of the casserole dish. Place the crust over the filled casserole and crimp the edges. Prick holes in the top with a fork. Bake until the filling is hot and bubbling and the crust is browned, about 45 minutes.

Sun-Butter Macaroni Pie

Loaded with protein and great flavor, this is a fun version of mac and cheese that kids will love. For a variation, substitute cooked small broccoli florets, Brussels sprouts, or asparagus pieces for the peas. To make this gluten-free, use gluten-free pasta and bread crumbs.

Cook the macaroni in a pot of salted boiling water until al dente, about 8 minutes. Drain and set aside in a lightly oiled baking dish or a 10-inch deep-dish pie plate.

Preheat the oven to 375°F. Heat 1 tablespoon of the oil or the water in a medium-size skillet over medium heat. Add the onion, cover, and cook until tender, about 5 minutes.

In a blender or food processor, combine the cooked onion, almond milk, tofu, sunflower seed butter, lemon juice, salt, mustard, cayenne, and nutmeg. Blend until smooth. Taste and adjust the seasonings, if needed.

Pour the sauce over the reserved macaroni, add the peas and parsley, and mix well.

In a small bowl, combine the bread crumbs and sunflower seeds with the remaining 1 tablespoon oil, stirring to coat. Sprinkle the crumbs onto the macaroni mixture, along with a few shakes of paprika, if using.

Cover and bake until hot and bubbly, about 25 minutes. Uncover and bake until the top is lightly browned, about 10 minutes longer.

Gluten Free

Serves 4

8 ounces elbow macaroni
1 to 2 tablespoons olive oil or 1/4 cup water
1 large yellow onion, chopped
2 cups plain unsweetened almond milk
4 ounces silken tofu
1/4 cup sunflower seed butter (page 7)
1 tablespoon fresh lemon juice
1/2 teaspoon salt
1/4 teaspoon mustard powder
Pinch cayenne
Pinch nutmeg
3/4 cup thawed frozen green peas
2 tablespoons minced fresh parsley
1/4 cup bread crumbs
1/4 cup ground sunflower seeds
Paprika (optional)

Szechuan Stir-Fry with Fiery Peanut Sauce

Serves 6

1/2 cup water
1/4 cup peanut butter (page 7)
1/4 cup wheat-free tamari
2 tablespoons rice vinegar
2 teaspoons natural sugar
1 teaspoon ketchup
1 clove garlic, minced
1 teaspoon grated fresh ginger
1 teaspoon red pepper flakes, or
　to taste
1 teaspoon cornstarch dissolved in
　1 tablespoon water
1 tablespoon neutral vegetable oil
8 ounces extra-firm tofu, drained,
　pressed, and cut into 1/2-inch
　strips
1 large yellow onion, halved length-
　wise and thinly sliced
2 cups broccoli florets, blanched
1 red bell pepper, cut into thin
　strips
2 cups thinly sliced napa cabbage
1 cup thinly sliced fresh shiitake
　mushrooms
4 cups cooked brown rice
1/4 cup roasted peanuts, chopped
　(optional)

Vary the vegetables according to your personal taste and their availability. The amount of heat in this dish can be controlled by the amount of red pepper flakes added. Strips of extra-firm tofu are a pleasant foil for the spicy sauce.

In a bowl, a food processor, or a blender, combine the water, peanut butter, tamari, vinegar, sugar, ketchup, garlic, ginger, and red pepper flakes, and blend well.

Pour the mixture into a saucepan and bring to a boil. Reduce the heat to low and simmer for 5 minutes, stirring occasionally. Add the cornstarch mixture and cook, stirring, until the sauce thickens. Remove from the heat and set aside.

Heat the oil in a large skillet or wok over medium-high heat. Add the tofu and stir-fry until golden brown, about 3 minutes. Remove with a slotted spoon and set aside. Add the onion, broccoli, and bell pepper, and stir-fry for 3 minutes. Add the cabbage and mushrooms and stir-fry 3 minutes longer, or until the vegetables soften, adding a little water if the vegetables start to stick.

Return the tofu to the skillet. Add the sauce and stir-fry to coat the vegetables. Serve over the rice and top with the chopped peanuts, if using.

Sweet and Spicy Stuffed Peppers

Salsa and pumpkin seed butter join forces in these colorful stuffed peppers that are a little spicy, a little sweet, and one-hundred percent delicious.

Preheat the oven to 350°F. Slice off the tops of the peppers, reserve and set aside. Remove the seeds and membranes of the peppers. Plunge the peppers into a pot of boiling water and cook until softened, about 5 minutes. Remove from the water and drain, cut side down. Chop the pepper tops and set aside.

Heat the oil or water in a large skillet over medium heat. Add the onion and reserved chopped pepper tops and cook until softened, about 5 minutes.

In a large bowl, combine the onion mixture with the rice, beans, salsa, pumpkin seed butter, jalapeños, parsley, sugar, and salt and pepper to taste. Mix well.

Fill the pepper cavities evenly with the rice mixture, packing tightly. Top with the pepitas. Place upright in a baking dish. Add the apple juice to the baking dish, cover tightly, and bake until the peppers are tender and the stuffing is hot, about 45 minutes.

Gluten Free
Soy Free

Serves 4

4 large red bell peppers
1 tablespoon olive oil or 1/4 cup water
1 small yellow onion, chopped
2 cups cooked white or brown rice
1 1/2 cups cooked or one 15.5-ounce can dark red kidney beans, drained and rinsed
1 cup tomato salsa
1/4 cup pumpkin seed butter (page 7)
2 tablespoons minced canned or jarred jalapeños
1 tablespoon minced fresh parsley
1 teaspoon natural sugar
Salt and ground black pepper
2 tablespoons chopped pepitas (hulled pumpkin seeds)
1/2 cup apple juice or water

Buckwheat Noodles with Ginger-Peanut Spinach

Gluten Free
Soy-Free Option

Serves 4

1/3 cup peanut butter (page 7)
1 clove garlic, minced
2 teaspoons grated fresh ginger
1 teaspoon natural sugar
3 tablespoons fresh lemon juice
2 tablespoons wheat-free tamari
1 cup water
1 tablespoon neutral vegetable oil
  or 1/4 cup water
9 ounces baby spinach
Salt and ground black pepper
12 ounces buckwheat soba noodles

Baby spinach, widely available in supermarkets, cooks quickly for a nourishing and delicious meal that can be on the table in minutes. If you have a gluten sensitivity, check to be sure your buckwheat soba noodles are 100% gluten free. For soy-free, use coconut aminos instead of tamari.

In a food processor, combine the peanut butter, garlic, ginger, and sugar. Add the lemon juice, tamari, and 1/2 cup of the water. Blend until smooth. Transfer the mixture to a saucepan and stir in the remaining 1/2 cup water. Heat over low heat, stirring until it is hot. Keep it warm.

Heat the oil or water in a large skillet over medium high heat, add the spinach, and sauté until wilted, about 1 minute. Season with salt and pepper to taste.

Cook the soba noodles according to package directions. Drain and rinse well, then transfer to a serving bowl. Add the spinach and the peanut sauce, and toss gently to combine. Serve hot.

Broccoli and Rice Noodles with Hoisin-Cashew Sauce

Deliciously rich and satisfying, chewy rice noodles combine with crisp vegetables and a fragrant, creamy sauce of cashews, hoisin sauce, lime, and cilantro. Use linguine if rice noodles are unavailable. Be sure to use a wheat-free tamari sauce to keep this gluten-free.

Soak the noodles in water for 15 minutes. Drain and set aside.

In a bowl or food processor, combine the cashew butter, hoisin sauce, garlic, tamari, lime juice, sugar, cayenne, and the 1/2 cup water. Blend until smooth. Add a little more water if needed for a creamy saucy consistency. Set aside.

Heat the oil or water in a skillet over medium-high heat. Add the onion and bell pepper and stir-fry until crisp-tender, 2 to 3 minutes. Add the reserved sauce, reduce the heat to low, and simmer until the sauce is hot. Keep warm.

In a large pot of boiling water, cook the rice noodles just until tender. Drain, rinse, and return to the pot. Add the sauce and toss to combine. Serve garnished with cilantro and cashews.

NOTE: If you are using fresh rice noodles, omit the soaking instructions.

Gluten Free

Serves 4

8 ounces flat dried rice noodles
1/2 cup cashew butter (page 7)
1/3 cup hoisin sauce
1 clove garlic, minced
2 tablespoons wheat-free tamari
1 tablespoon fresh lime juice
1 teaspoon natural sugar
1/4 teaspoon cayenne
1/2 cup water
1 tablespoon neutral vegetable oil or 1/4 cup water
1 small red onion, thinly sliced
1 small red bell pepper, seeded and thinly sliced
2 tablespoons minced fresh cilantro
2 tablespoons chopped roasted cashews

7 Sandwiches

My Favorite PB&J

Gluten-Free Option
Soy Free

Serves 2

4 slices whole grain or sprouted
  bread
1/4 cup peanut butter (page 7)
1/4 cup lime marmalade

Ever since my friend Sam introduced me to the joys of using lime marmalade to make a PB&J, I haven't looked back. In addition to contributing to a stellar PB&J, it's fabulous to use in sauces where a bit of sweet citrus flavor might be welcome. Use a gluten-free bread to make this gluten-free. Look for Rose's brand lime marmalade online. If you can't find it, substitute your favorite jam, jelly, or marmalade.

Spread 2 slices of the bread with the peanut butter.

Spread the remaining 2 slices of bread with the marmalade and place them on top of the peanut butter slices, filling sides in. Slice diagonally.

Flower Power Almond Butter Sandwich

Soy Free
Gluten-Free Option

Serves 2

1/2 cup almond butter (page 7)
1/4 cup finely shredded carrot
2 tablespoons sunflower seeds
2 tablespoons raisins
2 teaspoons pure maple syrup
  (optional)
4 slices whole grain or sprouted
  bread

Sunflower seeds add crunch to this nutritional almond butter powerhouse made with whole grain bread, raisins, and carrots. The optional maple syrup adds just a hint of sweetness. Use a gluten-free bread to make this gluten-free.

In a small bowl, combine the almond butter, carrot, sunflower seeds, raisins, and maple syrup, if using. Blend well.

Spread the almond butter mixture on 2 slices of the bread. Top each with the remaining 2 bread slices. Cut diagonally.

Grilled Peanut Butter and Banana Sandwich

Celebrate Elvis's birthday on January 8 with his favorite sandwich, and eat it the way he reportedly did: with a knife and fork. This sandwich is easy to double, infinitely versatile — substitute any kind of nut butter for the peanut butter, use jam or preserves in place of the bananas. Use a gluten-free bread to make this gluten-free.

Place the bananas in a bowl and mash them with a fork. Set aside.

Spread the butter on each slice of bread and place them, butter side down, on a flat work surface. Spread the peanut butter on 2 slices of the bread and the mashed banana on top of the peanut butter. Top with the remaining 2 bread slices, butter side up.

Cook the sandwiches on a griddle or large nonstick skillet over medium heat, turning once, until golden brown on both sides, about 4 minutes. Cut diagonally and serve.

Gluten-Free Option
Soy Free

Serves 2

2 small ripe bananas
1 tablespoon vegan butter
4 slices white or wholegrain bread
1/4 cup peanut butter (page 7)

A LOT OF SANDWICHES

Before the age of 18, the average American child consumes 1,500 peanut butter-and-jelly sandwiches.

Chocolate-Hazelnut Panini Sandwiches

Soy Free
Gluten-Free Option

Serves 4

CHOCOLATE-HAZELNUT BUTTER:
1 cup hazelnut butter (page 7)
3 tablespoons confectioners' sugar
3 tablespoons unsweetened cocoa
   powder
1/2 teaspoon vanilla extract

PANINIS:
8 slices good quality bread
2 tablespoons vegan butter, room
   temperature
1/2 cup raspberry jam or preserves
   (optional)

A popular spread, called Nutella, is made with hazlenuts and chocolate and is based on an old Italian recipe known as gianduja. Nutella isn't vegan, however you can find vegan spreads made with hazelnuts and chocolate, such as Justin's brand. If you prefer to make your own spread, look no further than this recipe in which a chocolate-hazelnut spread is the basis for these decadent paninis. Variations include swapping in another flavor of jam or adding sliced bananas to the sandwich. Use gluten-free bread to make this gluten-free.

CHOCOLATE-HAZELNUT BUTTER: In a food processor combine the hazelnut butter, sugar, cocoa, and vanilla. Process until well blended. It should be a spreadable consistency. If it is not, heat 1 to 2 tablespoons of almond milk in the microwave, and add to the mixture. Process until smooth and well blended. Transfer the spread to a bowl and set aside.

PANINIS: Butter the bread slices on 1 side with butter and place them on a flat work surface, butter side down. Spread 4 slices with 2 tablespoons of the chocolate-hazelnut butter. Spread the remaining slices with the jam (if using), and place them, jam side down, on top of the slices with the chocolate-hazelnut spread. Press them gently to flatten them slightly, buttered sides out.

In a panini press: Preheat a panini press to 375°F according to the manufacturer's instructions. Place a sandwich in the panini press and cook according to the manufacturer's instructions until golden brown and nicely toasted, 3 to 5 minutes. Repeat with remaining sandwiches.

In a skillet: Preheat a cast iron or non stick pan over medium heat. Add your sandwich, then press a heavy pan on top to weigh it down. Cook until golden and crisp, 3 to 4 minutes per side.

Repeat with remaining sandwiches.

TO SERVE: Cut the sandwiches in half crosswise. Serve immediately.

HAZELNUTS

Hazelnuts make a grainy, thick flavorful butter. Whole nuts need to be roasted in a 400° oven for 5 minutes to loosen the skins. Then enclose the nuts in a clean dishtowel and rub together to remove the skins.

Roasted Eggplant Pita with Garlicky Lemon-Almond Sauce

Serves 2

1 medium-size eggplant, trimmed
1 tablespoon olive oil
Salt and ground black pepper
3 tablespoons almond butter (page 7)
2 tablespoons fresh lemon juice
1 tablespoon wheat-free tamari
1 clove garlic, minced
1/4 teaspoon cayenne, or to taste
2 large pita loaves, halved
1 cup shredded romaine lettuce

This yummy sandwich filling is inspired by baba ghanoush, a Middle Eastern eggplant spread made with sesame butter or tahini. If you prefer to use an eggplant spread instead of the sliced eggplant, cut the eggplant in half lengthwise and roast, cut side down, on a lightly oiled baking sheet until soft, then scoop out the middle and add it to the almond butter mixture. For soy-free, use coconut aminos instead of tamari. For gluten-free, use gluten-free pitas.

Preheat the oven to 425°F. Quarter the eggplant lengthwise, then cut each quarter crosswise into 1/4-inch-thick slices. Arrange the eggplant slices on a lightly oiled baking sheet and brush with the olive oil. Sprinkle with salt and pepper to taste and bake, turning once, until softened and browned on both sides, about 15 minutes.

In a bowl or food processor, combine the almond butter, lemon juice, tamari, garlic, and cayenne. Blend until smooth.

Allow the eggplant to cool, then mix into the sauce. Stuff the pitas with the lettuce and the eggplant mixture and serve at once.

Peach-Almond Butter Quesadillas

Almond butter stands in for the peanut butter and peach jam replaces the classic grape jelly in this new spin on the classic PB & J. But that's not all: tortillas replace the bread to make delicious quesadillas. Variations are endless so feel free to use different combinations of nut butter and jam or other spread. Sliced bananas or fried vegan bacon slices make good additions. This recipe is easily doubled. For gluten-free, use gluten-free tortillas.

Spread one side of each of the tortillas evenly with the almond butter and peach jam.

Fold the tortillas in half to enclose the spreads. Place both quesadillas in a large non-stick skillet and cook until lightly browned on both sides, turning once.

To serve transfer the quesadillas to a cutting board and cut them into wedges.

Gluten- Free Option
Soy Free

Serves 2

2 (8-inch) flour tortillas
1/3 cup almond butter (page 7)
1/3 cup peach jam

GIANT SANDWICH

The world's largest peanut butter and jelly sandwich weighed close to 900 pounds. It contained 144 pounds of jelly, 350 pounds of peanut butter, and 400 pounds of bread. It was created in Oklahoma City, Oklahoma. The sandwich was made by Oklahoma Peanut Commission and the Oklahoma Wheat Commission to spotlight Oklahoma's top crops – peanuts and wheat.

Nutty Buddy Burgers

Gluten-Free Option
Soy-Free Option

Serves 4 to 6

1 small yellow onion, coarsely
    chopped
2 cloves garlic
1/2 cup peanuts, almonds, or ca-
    shews
1/2 cup walnuts or pecans
1/4 cup sunflower seeds
1 cup cooked lentils, well drained
1/4 cup dried bread crumbs
3 tablespoons nut butter (any kind)
    (page 7)
2 tablespoons wheat-free tamari
1 tablespoon minced fresh parsley
1/4 teaspoon cayenne (optional)
1 tablespoon olive oil

Three kinds of nut and seed buddies share the spotlight in these tasty burgers. You can change up their flavor by adding different spices or herbs. While you can serve the burgers on a roll or in a wrap with your favorite trimmings, they're even better served plated and topped with a mushroom sauce, chutney, or salsa. To make them soy-free, use coconut aminos instead of tamari. For gluten-free, use gluten-free bread crumbs.

Preheat the oven to 350°F. In a food processor, combine the onion, garlic, peanuts, walnuts, and sunflower seeds, pulsing to blend while leaving some texture. Add the lentils, bread crumbs, nut butter, tamari, parsley, and cayenne, if using. Pulse until the mixture is well combined. Shape the mixture into 4 large or 6 smaller patties and transfer to a platter. Refrigerate for 30 minutes.

Heat the oil in a skillet over medium heat, add the patties, and cook until browned on both sides, turning once, about 4 minutes per side.

VARIATION: Instead of cooking the burgers on top of the stove, they may be baked in the oven. To do so, arrange them on a lightly oiled baking sheet and bake at 350°F, turning once, until browned on both sides, about 25 to 30 minutes.

Thai Tofu-Vegetable Wraps

These wraps envelop crisp fresh vegetables and a zesty sauce for a yummy lunch or a light supper. To make this gluten-free, use gluten-free flatbreads.

Preheat the oven to 375°F. Lightly oil a baking sheet or spray it with cooking spray. Arrange the tofu strips on the pan, drizzle them with 1 tablespoon of the soy sauce, and season with salt and pepper to taste. Bake until lightly browned, turning once about halfway through, about 20 minutes total. Remove from the oven and set aside to cool.

In a small bowl, combine the cashew butter, tamari, lime juice, sugar, and chile paste. Blend well.

In a medium bowl, combine the lettuce, carrot, bell pepper, bean sprouts, if using, and onion. Toss to combine.

Spread the cashew mixture onto each flatbread, dividing evenly. Top with the vegetable mixture, spreading on the lower third of each wrap. Top the vegetables on each flatbread with strips of the reserved tofu.

Roll up the sandwiches and use a serrated knife to cut them in half. Serve at once.

Gluten-Free Option

Serves 2

8 ounces extra-firm tofu, cut into strips

2 tablespoons wheat-free tamari, divided

Salt and ground black pepper

3 tablespoons cashew butter (page 7)

1 tablespoon fresh lime juice

1 teaspoon natural sugar

1 teaspoon chili paste, or more to taste

1 cup shredded lettuce

1/2 cup shredded carrot

1/4 cup chopped red bell pepper

1/4 cup bean sprouts (optional)

2 tablespoons finely minced red onion or scallion

2 lavash flatbreads or large flour tortillas

Walnut Butter Waldorf Wraps

Serves 4

2 Gala or Fuji apples, peeled and
   cored
1 tablespoon fresh lemon juice
1/3 cup golden raisins
1/2 cup finely minced celery
2 scallions, finely minced
1/2 cup chopped toasted walnuts
1/3 cup walnut butter (page 7)
1/4 cup vegan mayonnaise
1/2 teaspoon natural sugar (optional)
Salt and ground black pepper
4 (7-inch) flour tortillas
1 cup shredded iceberg lettuce

The classic Waldorf salad gets a new look – made with walnut butter and wrapped inside a soft tortilla. I like a sweeter apple in this recipe such as Fuji, Delicious, or Gala. For soy-free, use a soy-free mayo. For gluten-free, use gluten-free tortillas.

Shred the apples or cut them into thin slices and place them in a large bowl. Add the lemon juice and toss to coat. Drain the liquid from the apples, then add the raisins, celery, scallions, and nuts.

In a small bowl, combine the walnut butter, mayonnaise, and sugar, if using, until blended. Spoon just enough of the dressing into the apple mixture to bind the ingredients together, stirring to mix well. Season to taste with salt and pepper. Reserve the remaining dressing to spread on the tortillas.

Place the tortillas on a flat work surface and spread the remaining dressing on them. Divide the apple mixture across the lower third of each tortilla, along with the shredded lettuce.

Roll up the sandwiches and use a serrated knife to cut them in half.

Open-Face Peanut Butter and Tomato Broil

Hot and tasty, this open-face sandwich is a sophisticated way to enjoy peanut butter. For a "PB&T" sandwich with more zing, top the peanut butter with spicy hot tomato salsa instead of the tomato slices. Use gluten-free English muffins to make this gluten-free.

Preheat the broiler. Spread the cut sides of the muffins with the peanut butter and place cut side up on a baking sheet.

Top each muffin half with a tomato slice and season with salt and pepper to taste. Place under the broiler until hot and lightly browned, about 2 minutes. Serve at once.

Soy Free
Gluten-Free Option

Serves 2

2 English muffins, split
1/4 cup peanut butter (page 7)
4 slices large ripe tomato
Salt and ground black pepper

EARLY ORIGINS OF PEANUT BUTTER

The origin of peanut butter can be traced to several different regions of the world. In China, creamy peanut sauces have been around for centuries, while records show that in Africa, peanuts have been ground for stews since at least the 15th century. In America, a creamy peanut porridge was served to soldiers during the Civil War. Peanuts were called goobers then – hence the popular anthem at the time, "Eating Goober Peas."

SANDWICHES UNLIMITED

Not long ago, the only nut butter sandwich around was the traditional PB&J made with peanut butter, grape jelly, and white bread. These days, you can choose from over a dozen kinds of nut butters. They can be paired with an orchard full of jams, jellies, preserves, and marmalades, and served on a wide variety of whole-grain breads. You can also get even more creative by adding another flavor layer to your sandwich filling by sprinkling your spreads with anything from dried or fresh fruits, to crushed nuts or chocolate, or even shredded carrots or cooked vegan bacon.

If you choose one ingredient from column A, one from column B, add one from column C, and then put them all on one of the choices from column D, you could potentially enjoy more than 32,130 different variations of America's favorite sandwich.

A	B	C	D
Nut Butter	**Sweet Spreads**	**Optional Add-Ons**	**Bread of Choice**
Peanut butter	Grape jelly	Raisins	Whole-grain bread
Almond butter	Peach jam	Dried cranberries	Gluten-free bread
Cashew butter	Strawberry preserves	Dried blueberries	Tortilla
Macadamia butter	Lime marmalade	Sliced bananas	Pita
Walnut butter	Orange marmalade	Grated chocolate	Bagel
Pecan butter	Apricot preserves	Crushed nuts	Lavash
Pistachio butter	Cherry jam	Minced celery	Baguette
Brazil nut butter	Blackberry jam	Shredded carrot	English muffin
Hazelnut butter	Apple jelly	Thinly-sliced cucumber	Bagel
Chestnut butter	Fig jam	Cooked vegan bacon	
Soy nut butter	Raspberry jam	Sliced apple	
Sesame butter	Blueberry preserves	Sliced pear	
Sunflower seed butter	Pineapple jam	Sliced peach	
Pumpkin seed butter	Guava jam	Ground flaxseeds	
	Mango jam	Vegan cream cheese	
	Red pepper jelly		
	Quince jelly		

8 Breakfast & Beyond

Mushroom-Cashew Breakfast Burritos

Gluten-Free Option
Soy Free

Serves 4

1 tablespoon olive oil or 1/4 cup water or vegetable broth
1 small yellow onion, chopped
2 garlic cloves minced
8 ounces cremini mushrooms, thinly sliced
8 ounces extra-firm tofu, drained, pressed, and crumbled
1/2 teaspoon dried thyme
Salt and black pepper
1/2 cup vegetable broth
1/3 cup cashew butter (page 7)
1 1/2 cups almond milk
4 (7-inch) soft tortillas, warmed
2 tablespoons minced fresh parsley

This makes a hearty breakfast, brunch, or light supper. Instead of making burritos, you can spoon the filling over toast or your favorite cooked grain or noodles. Use gluten-free tortillas to make this gluten-free.

Heat the oil or water in a large skillet over medium heat. Add the onion and cook until softened, about 5 minutes. Add the garlic and mushrooms and cook 2 minutes longer, stirring, until softened.

Stir in the tofu, thyme, and salt and pepper to taste and cook 1 minute longer, then stir in the broth, cashew butter, and almond milk, and cook until hot and slightly thickened, stirring frequently, about 10 minutes. Taste and adjust the seasonings, if needed.

To serve, scoop the mushroom and tofu mixture into the tortillas, roll up, and arrange on serving plates. Top with remaining filling and sauce and sprinkle with the parsley. Serve hot.

Oatmeal with a Swirl of Almond Butter

When is oatmeal more than just oatmeal? When it is enhanced by the creamy taste of almond butter for a nutrient-rich, stick-to-your-ribs breakfast. If you're gluten-sensitive, make sure your oats are gluten-free.

Bring the water to a boil in a medium saucepan over high heat. Reduce the heat to low and stir in the oats, cinnamon, and salt. Simmer for 5 minutes, stirring occasionally.

Remove from the heat, cover, and let stand for 2 to 3 minutes.

In a small saucepan, combine the almond butter, maple syrup, and almond milk over medium-low heat, stirring to blend.

To serve, spoon the oatmeal into 4 bowls and garnish each with a swirl of the almond butter mixture.

Gluten Free
Soy Free

Serves 4

4 cups water
2 cups old-fashioned rolled oats
3/4 teaspoon ground cinnamon
Pinch of salt
1/4 cup almond butter (page 7)
2 tablespoons pure maple syrup
1 tablespoon almond milk

Maple-Pecan Butter Waffles with Pecan Maple Syrup

Gluten-Free Option
Soy-Free Option

Serves 4

1/2 cup pecan butter (page 7)
2 tablespoons vegan butter
1 1/4 cups almond milk
1/4 cup pure maple syrup
1 teaspoon vanilla extract
1 1/2 cups all-purpose flour
3 teaspoons baking powder
1/4 teaspoon salt

Treat yourself to these yummy waffles, and top with the Pecan Maple Syrup to amplify the flavors. For gluten-free, use gluten-free flour. For soy-free, use soy-free vegan butter.

In a large bowl, cream together the pecan butter and butter. Add the milk, maple syrup, and vanilla and blend until smooth.

In a separate bowl, sift together the flour, baking powder, and salt. Add to the pecan butter mixture and stir until smooth.

Preheat the oven to 200°F. Preheat a waffle maker. Pour about 3/4 cup of the batter onto the waffle maker, spreading toward the edges if necessary, and cook according to manufacturer's instructions. Repeat until the remaining batter is used up. Keep the cooked waffles warm in the oven while preparing the rest.

Pecan Maple Syrup

Gluten Free
Soy-Free Option

Makes 3/4 cup

1/2 cup pure maple syrup
1/4 cup pecan butter (page 7)
1 tablespoon vegan butter

This richly decadent syrup, perfect with the waffles, is also great on ice cream. Use soy-free vegan butter or softened coconut oil to make this soy-free.

In a small saucepan over low heat, combine the maple syrup, pecan butter, and butter, stirring frequently until warm and well blended.

Apple-Almond Butter Pancakes

Apple slices with nut butter are a great healthy snack. Now, this delicious flavor combo can be enjoyed in these luscious pancakes. For gluten-free, use gluten-free flour. This recipe makes eight pancakes.

In a large bowl, combine the flour, sugar, baking powder, and salt.

In a blender, combine the milk, apple juice, almond butter, and vanilla and blend until smooth.

Pour into the flour mixture, stirring with a few swift strokes until just moist. Fold in the chopped apple and almonds.

Preheat the oven to 200°F. Lightly oil a griddle or nonstick skillet and heat until hot. Ladle about 1/4 cup of the batter onto the griddle or skillet. Cook on one side until small bubbles appear on the top of the pancakes, about 2 minutes.

Flip the pancakes with a spatula and cook until the second side is lightly browned, about 1 minute longer. Repeat with the remaining batter. Keep the cooked pancakes warm in the oven while preparing the remaining pancakes.

Gluten-Free Option
Soy Free

Serves 4

1 1/2 cups all-purpose flour
1 tablespoon natural sugar
2 teaspoons baking powder
1/4 teaspoon salt
1 1/2 cups almond milk
1/2 cup apple juice
3 tablespoons almond butter (page 7)
1 teaspoon vanilla extract
1 large apple, peeled, cored, and chopped
2 tablespoons chopped roasted almonds

Cranberry-Pecan Butter Muffins

Gluten-Free Option
Soy Free

Makes 12

1 tablespoon ground flaxseeds
3 tablespoons water
1/3 cup pecan butter (page 7)
3 tablespoons neutral vegetable oil
1 cup almond milk
1/2 cup natural sugar
1 3/4 cups all-purpose flour
2 1/2 teaspoons baking powder
1/2 teaspoon salt
3/4 teaspoon ground cinnamon
1/4 teaspoon ground allspice
3/4 cup dried sweetened cranberries
1/2 cup chopped pecans

The only thing better than savoring the aroma of these fresh-baked fragrant muffins is biting into one. Bejeweled with sweet-tart cranberries, and loaded with protein and calcium, they are a good choice for breakfast or a between-meal snack served with coffee or tea. For gluten-free, use a gluten-free flour. For a less sweet muffin, use 1/3 cup of sugar.

Preheat the oven to 400°F. Lightly grease a muffin pan.

Combine the flaxseeds and water in a blender and blend until thickened, about 1 minute. Set aside.

In a large bowl, combine the pecan butter and oil. Add the milk, flaxseed mixture, and sugar and blend until smooth.

In a separate bowl, combine the flour, baking powder, salt, cinnamon, and allspice. Stir into the pecan butter mixture until just blended.

Fold in the cranberries, then transfer the batter into the prepared muffin pan, filling the cups about two-thirds full. Sprinkle the tops with about 2 teaspoons of chopped pecans.

Bake until golden brown and a toothpick inserted into a muffin comes out clean, 15 to 18 minutes. Cool in the pan for 5 to 10 minutes. Serve warm.

Ginger-Walnut Scones

These scones taste best when eaten on the same day they are made. For a more pronounced ginger-walnut flavor, add some finely minced crystallized ginger and chopped roasted walnuts to the dough. For gluten-free, use a gluten-free flour. For soy-free, use a soy-free vegan butter.

Preheat the oven to 400°F. Lightly grease and flour a baking sheet.

In a large bowl, combine the flour, sugar, baking powder, baking soda, ginger, and salt. Cut the vegan butter and walnut butter into the flour mixture until it is crumbly. Mix in the almond milk, vanilla, and walnut pieces, stirring until just blended. Do not overmix.

Transfer the dough to a lightly floured surface and pat the dough into a 1-inch thick circle. Cut the dough into 12 wedges and place them on a lightly greased baking sheet. Bake until golden brown, 18 to 20 minutes. Serve warm.

Gluten-Free Option
Soy-Free Option

Makes 12 scones

2 cups unbleached all-purpose flour
1/2 cup natural sugar
2 teaspoons baking powder
1 teaspoon baking soda
1 teaspoon ground ginger
1/2 teaspoon salt
1/3 cup vegan butter
1/3 cup walnut butter (page 7)
1/4 cup almond milk
1 teaspoon pure vanilla extract
1/3 cup chopped walnut pieces

WALNUT TIP

Soft, rich walnut butter can have a slightly bitter taste. This can be avoided if you roast the walnuts before making them into nut butter.

Walnut Butter Banana Bread

Makes 1 loaf

1 cup almond milk
1 cup natural sugar
3/4 cup walnut butter (page 7)
1 teaspoon vanilla extract
2 large ripe bananas, chopped
2 1/4 cups all-purpose flour
2 teaspoons baking powder
1 teaspoon cinnamon
1/4 teaspoon salt
1/2 cup chopped roasted walnuts

One taste will tell you this isn't your everyday banana bread. This recipe has the added goodness of creamy walnut butter and chopped roasted walnuts. For a fun and delicious variation, add 1/2 cup vegan chocolate chips to the batter. For gluten-free, use a gluten-free flour.

Preheat the oven to 350°F. Generously oil a 9 x 5-inch loaf pan and set it aside.

In a blender or food processor, combine the milk, sugar, walnut butter, vanilla, and 1 banana, and blend until smooth.

In a large bowl, sift together the flour, baking powder, cinnamon, and salt. Add the banana mixture and mix well. Fold in the walnuts and the remaining banana.

Fill the prepared pan with the batter and bake until a toothpick inserted into the center comes out clean, about 1 hour. Cool in the pan before slicing.

Handcrafted Granola Sunflower Bars

Easy to make and loaded with flavor, you can customize these granola bars to include your favorite ingredients. For example, you can substitute any kind of chopped nuts for the sunflower seeds or peanuts, or swap out a different kind of nut butter in place of the peanut butter. It is important that you use ground flaxseeds, available at natural food stores. If you buy whole flaxseeds, you can grind them at home in a spice grinder. If you're gluten-sensitive, be sure your oats are gluten-free. For soy-free, use a soy-free vegan butter.

Preheat the oven to 325°F. Lightly grease an 8-inch square baking pan.

In a large mixing bowl, combine the oats, sunflower seeds, flaxseeds, peanuts, raisins, and coconut in a large bowl. Set aside.

In a saucepan, combine the maple syrup, peanut butter, butter, and sugar. Cook over medium heat, stirring constantly, until the sugar is dissolved and the mixture is smooth. Stir in the apple juice, vanilla, and baking soda, and remove from the heat.

Pour into the oats mixture and stir until well combined. Transfer the mixture into the prepared pan. Place a piece of plastic wrap on top and top with another pan or a book that will fit inside the baking pan to weight it down. Use your hands to press down on the weight firmly and evenly so that the mixture spreads evenly in the pan. Remove the weight and the plastic wrap and bake for 20 minutes. Cool to room temperature, then cover and refrigerate until firm. Use a sharp knife to cut into twelve (1 1/3- x 4-inch) bars and store them in the refrigerator for up to 2 weeks.

Gluten Free
Soy-Free Option

Makes 12

2 1/2 cups old-fashioned rolled oats
1 cup sunflower seeds
3/4 cup ground flaxseeds
1/2 cup chopped unsalted peanuts (or other chopped nuts)
1/2 cup raisins
1/2 cup flaked coconut
1/2 cup pure maple syrup
2/3 cup peanut or other nut butter (page 7)
1/3 cup vegan butter
1/3 cup natural sugar
1 tablespoon apple juice
2 teaspoons vanilla extract
1 teaspoon baking soda

Pineapple-Coconut Smoothie

....

Serves 1 or 2

1 large ripe banana, cut into
  chunks and frozen
1/2 cup fresh or canned pineapple
  chunks
3/4 cup coconut milk
2 tablespoons cashew butter (page 7)
1 teaspoon vanilla extract
3 to 4 ice cubes

Cashew butter adds richness and protein to this tropical smoothie. Smoothies are a great way to use bananas that are beginning to get too ripe. Just peel, cut into chunks, and store in the freezer. That way, you can have cold, rich smoothies at a moment's notice.

In a blender, combine the banana, pineapple, coconut milk, cashew butter, vanilla, and ice cubes. Blend until smooth. Serve immediately.

Peanut Butter and Banana Smoothie

....

Serves 1 or 2

2 large frozen ripe peeled bananas, cut into chunks
3/4 cup almond milk
2 tablespoons peanut butter (page 7)
1 teaspoon vanilla extract
4 ice cubes

The classic sandwich combo also makes a satisfying and energizing smoothie loaded with potassium from the bananas and protein from the almond milk and peanut butter.

In a blender, combine the bananas, almond milk, peanut butter, vanilla, and ice cubes. Blend until smooth. Serve immediately.

MAKE YOUR OWN FLAVORED NUT BUTTERS

If flavored nut butters appeal to you, there are some creative flavors available from a variety of nut butter companies. Among the luscious combinations are chocolate coconut peanut butter, maple almond butter, chia-infused peanut butter, cinnamon red maca almond butter, and coconut cardamom butter. Look online for where to buy a wide variety of flavored nut butters. Because these products can be expensive, you may choose to use them as inspiration to make your own combinations at home. Flavored nut butters are as easy to make as the plain varieties, and in addition to saving money, you can customize the flavors according to your own taste. Whether you prefer sweet or savory notes, or want to spice it up, you can use flavored nut butters to create unique sandwich spreads, dips, or to make delicious sauces to toss with noodles or vegetables.

To make flavored nut butters, begin by making a batch of basic nut butter of your choice. Then add your favorite seasonings to taste, and you're all set. There are no hard and fast rules to flavoring your nut butters – start by adding a small amount of your add-in ingredient to a batch of nut butter and taste as you go until you get the perfect flavor balance. Here are some ideas for sweet and savory additions to get you started:

- maple syrup or agave
- melted chocolate
- ground cinnamon or cardamom
- vanilla extract
- crystalized ginger
- fruit jam

- smoked paprika
- cayenne
- pureed garlic
- soy sauce
- curry or other or other spice blend

9 Desserts

Pineapple Coconut Cheesecake

Serves 8

1 cup almonds, soaked overnight,
  then drained and blotted dry
1/2 cup dried pineapple
3/4 cup shredded coconut
1 cup raw cashews, soaked overnight and drained
1 cup fresh or canned pineapple,
  drained well and blotted dry
16 ounces vegan cream cheese, at
  room temperature
1 cup natural sugar
2 tablespoons cornstarch
1 1/2 teaspoons fresh lemon juice
1 1/2 teaspoons coconut extract

The tropical flavors of coconut and pineapple are featured in this yummy cheesecake. For a piña colada variation, replace the lemon juice with rum extract.

Preheat the oven to 350°F. Grease an 8-inch springform pan and set aside. In a food processor, combine the drained soaked almonds, dried pineapple, and 1/4 cup of the shredded coconut, and process until finely ground. The mixture should stick together when pressed between your fingers. If it is too dry, add a few soft pitted dates or a tablespoon of pineapple juice or coconut milk and process until the mixture holds together. Spread the mixture in bottom of the prepared pan, and press it evenly into bottom and sides of pan. Bake the crust for 8 to 10 minutes then remove from the oven and set aside.

In a food processor or high-speed blender, combine the soaked and drained cashews, fresh pineapple, cream cheese, sugar, cornstarch, lemon juice, and coconut extract and blend until smooth and very creamy.

Pour the filling into the prepared crust and bake for 35 minutes. Remove from the oven and sprinkle the top with the remaining 1/2 cup coconut. Return to the oven for 10 minutes. Turn off the oven and leave the cheesecake inside for another 10 minutes.

Remove the cake from the oven and cool at room temperature, then refrigerate at least 4 hours before serving. Carefully remove the sides of the springform pan before slicing. (You may need to run a knife around the edge of the cake to separate it from the pan.) Cover and refrigerate any leftovers.

Lea's Pineapple Sauce

When Lea Jacobson tested the Pineapple Coconut Cheese-cake, she whipped up this quick and easy sauce as a topping for it. In addition to being delicious, it's a great way to use any extra pineapple you may have on hand from making the cheesecake.

Combine all the ingredients in a high-speed blender and blend until smooth.

Gluten Free
Soy Free

Makes 1 ½ cups

1 cup fresh or canned pineapple
  chunks
1/2 cup dried pineapple
1 tablespoon lemon juice or apple
  cider vinegar

KID'S NUT BUTTER PARTY

Here's a way to keep your kids and their friends occupied and provide a healthy snack at the same time: Have a nut butter sandwich-making contest. Put all the ingredients on a table: bread and tortillas, a few kinds of nut butter, a few jellies and jams, sliced fruit, raisins, potato chips, and anything else you want to include. Award prizes for the most creative, most nutritious, most unusual, etc. – and let the kids do the voting. Then let them eat what they made.

IMPORTANT: Check with parents to make sure none of the children invited to the gathering is allergic to nuts.

Summer Berry Cheesecake

Gluten Free
....

Serves 8

3/4 cup almonds, soaked overnight, then drained and blotted dry

3/4 cup soft pitted dates

1 cup raw cashews, soaked overnight, then drained and blotted dry

1/2 cup natural sugar

1 tablespoon fresh lemon juice

1 teaspoon vanilla extract

2 (8-ounce) containers vegan cream cheese, at room temperature

1 1/2 cups fresh or thawed frozen strawberries, blackberries, or raspberries, well drained and blotted dry

2 tablespoons cornstarch

Fresh berries and mint leaves, for garnish

This light and luscious cheesecake features your favorite berries of summer. The creamy goodness comes from cashews blended into a rich butter and combined with vegan cream cheese. Be sure your berries are well-drained and blotted dry to remove any liquid.

Grease an 8-inch springform pan and set aside. In a food processor, combine the drained soaked almonds and the dates and process until finely ground. Press the mixture into the bottom of the prepared pan. Set aside. Preheat the oven to 350°F.

In a food processor or high-speed blender, combine the soaked and drained cashews, sugar, lemon juice, and vanilla, and process to a paste. Add the cream cheese, berries, and cornstarch, and blend until smooth and very creamy.

Pour the filling into the prepared crust and bake for 45 minutes. Turn off the oven and leave the cheesecake inside for another 10 minutes.

Remove the cake from the oven and cool at room temperature, then refrigerate at least 4 hours before serving. Carefully remove the sides of the springform pan before slicing. (You may need to run a knife around the edge of the cake to separate it from the pan.) Serve garnished with fresh berries and mint. Cover and refrigerate any leftovers.

Chocolate-Peanut Butter Cheesecake

Peanut butter and chocolate have long been a winning combination. When they're joined in a cheesecake, the result is pure bliss. To make this gluten-free, use gluten-free cookie crumbs.

CRUST: Preheat the oven to 350°F. Lightly oil an 8-inch springform pan.

In a bowl or food processor, combine the crumbs with the butter and mix well. Place the crumb mixture in the bottom of the prepared pan and press it against the bottom and sides. Refrigerate until chilled.

FILLING: In a large bowl, combine 8 ounces of cream cheese, 1/2 cup of the sugar, 1/4 cup of the milk, and the peanut butter and beat until smooth. Pour into the prepared crust and set aside.

In the same bowl, combine the remaining 8 ounces of cream cheese, 1/4 cup sugar, and 1/4 cup milk and beat until smooth. Fold in the melted chocolate and mix until well blended.

Using a circular motion, pour the chocolate mixture into the peanut butter mixture. If desired, use a thin metal spatula or knife, swirl the different colored mixtures around to create a marbled pattern.

Bake until firm, about 50 minutes. Turn off the oven and let the cheesecake sit in the off oven for 10 minutes. Remove the cake from the oven and let it cool completely at room temperature. Refrigerate for several hours before serving.

Gluten-Free Option

Serves 8

CRUST:
1 1/2 cups chocolate cookie crumbs
1/4 cup vegan butter, melted

FILLING:
16 ounces vegan cream cheese, at room temperature
3/4 cup natural sugar, divided
1/2 cup almond milk, divided
1/3 cup peanut butter, at room temperature (page 7)
1/2 cup semisweet vegan chocolate chips, melted

Peach Pie with Hazelnut Crumb Topping

Gluten-Free Option
Soy-Free Option

Serves 8

CRUST:
1 cup all-purpose flour
1/2 teaspoon salt
1/3 cup vegan butter, cut into small pieces
2 tablespoons ice water, or more if needed

FILLING:
1 tablespoon all-purpose flour
6 fresh ripe peaches, peeled, pitted, and sliced
2 tablespoons natural sugar
1 teaspoon fresh lemon juice
1/4 teaspoon ground cinnamon
1/8 teaspoon ground allspice

TOPPING:
1/3 cup all-purpose flour
1/3 cup natural sugar
1/4 cup old-fashioned rolled oats
1/4 cup hazelnut butter (page 7)
1 tablespoon vegan butter, cut into small pieces
1/4 teaspoon ground cinnamon
1/8 teaspoon ground allspice

This pie is a delicious way to enjoy fresh ripe peaches. The crumb topping, made with hazelnut butter and rolled oats, is more healthful than using a double pie crust, so you won't feel guilty going back for seconds. If your peaches are not very sweet, you may want to add a little more sugar. To make this pie gluten-free, use gluten-free flour; for soy-free, use soy-free vegan butter.

CRUST: Combine the flour and salt in a bowl. Add the butter and use a pastry blender to mix until crumbly. Add enough ice water to form a dough, starting with 2 tablespoons and adding more if needed.

Roll out into a circle to fit a 9-inch pie plate. Arrange the dough in the pie plate, crimping the edges. Preheat the oven to 375°F.

FILLING: In a large bowl, combine the flour, peaches, sugar, lemon juice, cinnamon, and allspice.

Mix gently and pour into the prepared crust. Set aside.

TOPPING: In small bowl, combine the flour, sugar, oats, hazelnut butter, butter, cinnamon, and allspice. Use a pastry blender to mix until crumbly.

Sprinkle the topping over the peach mixture and bake until the fruit is bubbly and the topping is browned, 50 to 60 minutes. Serve warm or at room temperature.

Apple-Almond Butter Crumble

Try this homey dessert the next time you're in the mood for apple pie but don't want the labor of a pie crust. To make this gluten-free, use gluten-free flour and oats; for soy-free, use soy-free vegan butter.

In small bowl, combine 1/4 cup of the sugar, the oats, flour, almond butter, butter, and 1/2 teaspoon of the cinnamon. Use a pastry blender to mix until crumbly. Set aside.

Preheat the oven to 375°F. Peel, core, and thinly slice the apples and place them in a large bowl. Add the lemon juice, allspice, cornstarch, and the remaining 1/2 cup sugar, and 1/2 teaspoon cinnamon. Stir to mix well, then spoon the apple mixture into a shallow baking dish or 10-inch deep-dish pie plate. Sprinkle the reserved topping evenly over the apples.

Bake until the apples are tender and the topping is golden brown, about 45 minutes. Serve warm or at room temperature.

Gluten-Free Option
Soy-Free Option

Serves 8

3/4 cup natural sugar, divided
1/2 cup old-fashioned rolled oats
1/4 cup all-purpose flour
1/4 cup almond butter (page 7)
2 tablespoons vegan butter
1 teaspoon cinnamon, divided
4 large Granny Smith or other
  cooking apples
1 tablespoon fresh lemon juice
1/4 teaspoon allspice
1 tablespoon cornstarch

Black-Bottom Peanut Butter Freezer Pie

Gluten-Free Option
Soy-Free Option

Serves 8

CRUST:
1 1/2 cups vegan chocolate cookie crumbs
1/4 cup vegan butter, melted

FILLING:
1 quart vegan vanilla ice cream, softened
3/4 cup peanut butter (page 7)
1/4 cup chopped peanuts
1 cup chocolate curls

This richly decadent peanut butter pie is quick and easy to make, but looks and tastes like it took all day to prepare. To make this pie gluten-free, use gluten-free cookie crumbs; for soy-free, use soy-free vegan butter and ice cream.

CRUST: Lightly coat a 9-inch pie plate with nonstick cooking spray.

In a medium bowl, combine the cookie crumbs and the butter until well blended. Transfer to the prepared pan and press the crumb mixture onto the bottom and sides. Set aside.

FILLING: In a large bowl, combine the ice cream with the peanut butter, mixing until well blended. Spoon into the prepared crust. Freeze for 4 to 6 hours or overnight.

When ready to serve, let the pie sit at room temperature for 5 minutes. Sprinkle the chopped peanuts in the center of the pie and the chocolate curls along the outer edge.

Double-Dare Peanut Butter Cake

Peanut butter lovers will appreciate the double indulgence of this peanut butter cake topped with peanut butter frosting. To make these gluten-free, use gluten-free flour; for soy-free, use soy-free vegan butter.

CAKE: Preheat oven to 350°F. Lightly grease an 8-inch baking pan and set aside.

In a medium bowl, combine the flour, baking powder, and salt.

In a large bowl, using an electric mixer, cream together the peanut butter, butter, and sugar until blended. Beat in the almond milk and vanilla until blended. Add the flour mixture and mix on low speed until evenly blended.

Transfer the batter to the prepared pan and bake until done, about 30 minutes, or when a tester comes out clean. Let the cake cool completely before icing.

FROSTING: Combine the sugar, peanut butter, milk, butter, and vanilla in a food processor and blend until smooth and creamy.

Refrigerate at least 1 hour before using to allow it to firm up, then frost the cake and sprinkle the top with the chocolate curls, if using.

Gluten-Free Option
Soy-Free Option

Serves 8

CAKE:
1 1/2 cups unbleached all-purpose flour
2 teaspoons baking powder
1/4 teaspoon salt
3/4 cup peanut butter, at room temperature (page 7)
1/4 cup vegan butter, at room temperature
1 cup natural sugar
1/2 cup almond milk
1 teaspoon vanilla extract

FROSTING:
1 1/2 cups confectioners' sugar
1/2 cup creamy peanut butter
1/4 cup almond milk
3 tablespoons vegan butter, softened
1 teaspoon vanilla extract
1 cup chocolate curls (optional)

Nut Butter Fantasy Brownies

Gluten-Free Option
Soy-Free Option

Makes 9 brownies

1 large ripe banana, peeled
1/3 cup nut butter of choice (page 7)
1 teaspoon vanilla extract
4 ounces semisweet vegan
  chocolate
3/4 cup natural sugar
1/4 cup vegan butter
1 1/4 cups all-purpose flour
1 teaspoon baking powder
1/2 cup chopped roasted nuts of
  choice (one type or a combination)

The happy marriage of chocolate, bananas, and your favor-ite nut butter results in these rich, moist brownies. To make these gluten-free, use gluten-free flour; for soy-free, use soy-free vegan butter.

Preheat the oven to 350°F. Lightly grease the bottom only of an 8-inch square baking pan. Set aside.

In a blender or food processor, combine the banana, nut butter, and vanilla, and puree until smooth. Set aside.

Place the chocolate in a small heatproof bowl and melt over a small saucepan of simmering water, stirring occasionally, until melted. Keep warm over very low heat.

In a medium bowl, combine the sugar and butter and beat until well blended. Beat in the reserved banana mixture and blend well. Add the flour and baking powder and beat until combined.

Spoon the batter into the prepared pan, then swirl in the reserved chocolate to create a marbled effect. Sprinkle the nuts on top.

Bake until the top springs back when touched, about 30 minutes. Cool completely in the pan before cutting.

Pistachio Butter Biscotti

These biscotti make a nice, not-too-sweet accompaniment to a cup of coffee or tea in the afternoon. For a more decadent version, glaze the tops with melted chocolate. To make these gluten-free, use gluten-free flour; for soy-free, use soy-free vegan butter.

Preheat the oven to 350°F. Lightly oil a baking sheet.

In a mixing bowl, cream the sugar into the butter and pistachio butter until well blended. Blend in the almond milk and vanilla. Mix in the flour and baking powder, then stir in the chopped pistachios. Chill the dough for 10 minutes.

Form the dough into a slab about 1 inch high and place it on the prepared baking sheet. Flatten slightly. Bake until golden brown, 25 to 30 minutes, or until a toothpick inserted comes out clean. Remove from the oven and reduce the temperature to 300°F.

Cool for 10 minutes, then cut into 1/2-inch-thick slices. Place the sliced biscotti on their sides on an ungreased baking sheet and bake for 10 minutes. Cool completely before storing in an airtight container, where they will keep for up to 2 weeks.

Gluten-Free Option
Soy-Free Option

Makes 12 biscotti

2/3 cup natural sugar
1/3 cup vegan butter, softened
1/4 cup pistachio butter (page 7)
1/4 cup almond milk
1 teaspoon vanilla extract
2 cups all-purpose flour
2 teaspoons baking powder
1/4 cup chopped pistachios

PISTACHIO TIP

Because they contain less oil, pistachios make a slightly dry butter that can clump while processing. For a smoother butter, add a small amount of neutral vegetable oil during processing.

Three-Nut Butter Cookies

Gluten-Free Option
Soy-Free Option

Makes 3 dozen

2 cups unbleached all-purpose
   flour
1 teaspoon baking powder
1/2 teaspoon salt
1/2 cup almond butter (page 7)
1/3 cup walnut butter (page 7)
1/4 cup peanut butter (page 7)
2/3 cup natural sugar
1/2 cup vegan butter, softened
1 teaspoon vanilla extract
1/2 cup finely chopped toasted
   walnuts, almonds, and/or peanuts

If you don't have all three nut butters on hand, make this recipe using whatever one (or two) nut butters you do have. To make these gluten-free, use gluten-free flour and oats; for soy-free, use soy-free vegan butter.

Preheat oven to 350°F. In a medium bowl, combine the flour, baking powder, and salt.

In a bowl or food processor, combine the three nut butters, sugar, butter, and vanilla, and blend until smooth. Add to the flour mixture and stir briskly until just blended. Stir in the chopped nuts.

Pinch off a piece of the dough (about 2 tablespoons) and shape it into a ball. Place it onto a nonstick baking sheet. Repeat with the remaining dough, spacing them a few inches apart. With the tines of a fork, press lightly into the tops of the cookies to flatten them slightly.

Bake until lightly browned but still slightly soft, about 12 minutes. Cool completely before serving. Store in an airtight container.

Oatmeal-Pumpkin Seed Bars

These tasty treats are quick and easy to put together in the food processor and bake in just 20 minutes. To make these gluten-free, use gluten-free flour and oats; for soy-free, use soy-free vegan butter.

Preheat the oven to 350°F. Lightly grease an 8-inch square baking pan.

In a food processor, combine the butter, sugar, pumpkin seed butter, and vanilla until blended. Add the oats, flour, cranberries, and pumpkin seeds and pulse until well combined. Press the mixture into the bottom of the prepared pan and bake for 20 minutes.

Remove from the oven and drizzle with the melted chocolate, if using. Cool completely in the pan, then cut into 2 3/4- x 2-inch bars.

Gluten-Free Option
Soy-Free Option

Makes 12

1/2 cup vegan butter
1/2 cup natural sugar
1/3 cup pumpkin seed butter (page 7)
1 teaspoon vanilla extract
2 cups old-fashioned rolled oats
1/4 cup all-purpose flour
1/3 cup sweetened dried cranberries
1/4 cup chopped roasted hulled pumpkin seeds
4 ounces semisweet vegan chocolate chips, melted (optional)

BIBLICAL NUTS

The only nuts mentioned by name in the Bible are pistachios and almonds.

Almond Joy Pudding

Gluten Free
....
Serves 4

1 cup semisweet vegan chocolate
  chips
1/2 cup almond butter (page 7)
1/3 cup almond or coconut milk
6 ounces extra-firm silken tofu
1/4 cup maple syrup or agave
1 teaspoon coconut extract
1 teaspoon almond extract
2 tablespoons toasted coconut or
  slivered almonds

Coconut, almond, and chocolate combine in this luscious pudding that is a pure joy to eat. For an elegant presentation, serve in martini glasses garnished with toasted coconut and almond slivers or some chocolate curls and a ripe strawberry or a few raspberries. Alternately, pour the pudding into a prepared chocolate cookie crumb crust for a decadent pie.

Melt the chocolate in the top of a double boiler over gently simmering water, stirring frequently. Set aside.

In a high-speed blender or food processor, combine the almond butter, coconut milk, and tofu and process until smooth. Add the maple syrup, reserved melted chocolate, and coconut and almond extracts. Blend until smooth.

Transfer to individual dessert dishes, cover, and refrigerate until well chilled. When ready to serve, sprinkle the top of each dessert with some toasted coconut or almonds.

Lemon-Kissed Chocolate-Cashew Mousse

A touch of lemon adds a refreshing flavor note to this chocolatey rich mousse. A garnish of chopped cashews adds crunch.

Melt the chocolate in the top of a double boiler over gently simmering water, stirring frequently. Set aside.

In a dry blender, grind the cashews to a fine powder. Add the lemon juice, tofu, agave, and vanilla extract and blend until smooth. Add the reserved melted chocolate and 1 teaspoon of the lemon zest, and process until smooth.

Transfer to individual dessert dishes, cover, and refrigerate until well chilled.

When ready to serve, sprinkle the top of each dessert with the remaining lemon zest and chocolate curls or nuts.

Gluten Free

Serves 4

1 cup vegan semisweet chocolate chips
1/2 cup raw cashews
3 tablespoons fresh lemon juice
6 ounces extra-firm silken tofu, drained and blotted dry
1/4 cup agave nectar or maple syrup
1 teaspoon vanilla extract
2 teaspoons finely grated lemon zest, divided
2 tablespoons chocolate curls or toasted chopped cashews, for garnish

Coconut-Macadamia Wonton Cups with Fresh Mango

Soy Free

Serves 8

8 vegan wonton wrappers
Neutral vegetable oil
2 ripe mangoes
1 cup unsweetened coconut milk
1/2 cup natural sugar
1 1/2 tablespoons cornstarch dissolved in 2 tablespoons water
1/3 cup macadamia butter (page 7)
Mint leaves

The creamy filling is nestled in crisp wonton cups, studded with refreshing bits of mango, and garnished with sliced mango and mint, to create a dazzling and different dessert. Use ripe, sweet mangoes for the best results.

Preheat the oven to 375°F. Lightly brush the wonton wrappers on both sides with a small amount of oil. Gently press each wrapper into the cups of a muffin tin. Bake until lightly crisped, 6 to 8 minutes. Remove from the oven and set aside to cool.

Chop 1 mango and set aside. Cut the remaining mango into thin slices and set aside.

In a small saucepan, heat the coconut milk and sugar just to a boil, stirring to dissolve the sugar. Reduce the heat to low and stir in the cornstarch mixture, stirring to thicken. Add the macadamia butter and blend until smooth.

Transfer the mixture to a bowl and fold in the chopped mango. Refrigerate until chilled.

When ready to serve, spoon the chilled filling into the wonton cups and arrange on dessert plates. Garnish with the sliced mango and mint leaves.

Grilled Fruit Satays with Pineapple-Coconut Peanut Sauce

Vary the fruit according to the season and your preference – bananas, apricots, and peaches are good choices. If using bamboo skewers, be sure to soak them in water for 30 minutes to prevent burning. Use a soy-free vegan butter to make this soy-free.

SAUCE: Melt the butter in a small saucepan over medium heat. Add the sugar and stir to dissolve. Stir in the peanut butter, then add the pineapple juice and coconut milk, stirring constantly. Reduce the heat to low and simmer for 1 minute. Keep warm while you grill the fruit.

FRUIT: Thread the plums, pineapple, and strawberries onto skewers in an alternating pattern. Sprinkle with a little sugar and grill them on both sides, just until grill marks start to appear, about 5 minutes.

Arrange the skewered fruit on 4 plates along with small dipping bowls of the warm sauce.

Gluten Free
Soy-Free Option

Serves 4

SAUCE:
2 tablespoons vegan butter
1/2 cup natural sugar, plus more to sprinkle fruit
1/2 cup peanut butter (page 7)
1/2 cup pineapple juice
1/2 cup unsweetened coconut milk

FRUIT:
3 ripe plums, halved, pitted, and cut into 1 1/2-inch chunks
1 pineapple, peeled, cored, and cut into 1 1/2-inch chunks
1 cup hulled strawberries

10 Sweet Treats

Orange Decadence
Chocolate-Almond Truffles

Makes 24

1/2 cup almond butter (page 7)
1/4 cup vegan butter
2 cups confectioners' sugar
1/2 cup unsweetened cocoa
1 1/2 tablespoons Grand Marnier
   or other orange liqueur
1 tablespoon almond milk
1 teaspoon finely grated orange
   zest
3 tablespoons unsweetened cocoa
   (optional)

When you combine orange liqueur with chocolate and almond butter, the result is pure decadence. These luscious morsels are easy to make and sublimely delicious. Serve the truffles in gold foil paper candy cups for an elegant presentation.

In a food processor combine the almond butter, butter, sugar, cocoa, orange liqueur, almond milk, and orange zest. Process until well blended.

Shape the mixture into 1-inch balls and place them on a platter or a baking sheet. Roll in cocoa, if using.

Cover and refrigerate to firm up. Keep refrigerated until ready to use.

NUTS IN HISTORY

In 1899, Almeeta Lambert published the first nut cookbook, *The Complete Guide to Nut Cookery.*

Peanut Butter Cups

For bite-size versions of this delicious treat, use small paper candy cups instead of the cupcake liners. To make these soy-free, use a soy-free vegan butter.

Melt the butter in a medium-size saucepan over low heat. Stir in the peanut butter and vanilla until well blended. Remove from the heat and stir in the sugar. Mix well until thoroughly combined, then refrigerate.

Place the chocolate chips in a heatproof bowl and set it over a saucepan of simmering water until the chocolate is melted.

Use a small brush to coat the chocolate over the bottom and about 1/2 inch up the sides of 18 paper cupcake liners. Reserve the remaining chocolate. Refrigerate the cups until firm, about 10 minutes.

Scoop out about 1 1/2 tablespoons of the peanut butter mixture and shape into a ball. Flatten the ball into a disc and place inside one of the chilled chocolate-lined cups. Repeat until all the cups are filled. Spoon the remaining 2 teaspoons melted chocolate over the tops of each cup. Refrigerate until firm.

Variation: Use vegan white chocolate chips to make White Chocolate Peanut Butter Cups.

Soy-Free Option

Makes 18

1/2 cup vegan butter
1 cup peanut butter (page 7)
1/2 teaspoon vanilla extract
3/4 cup confectioners' sugar
16 ounces semisweet vegan
  chocolate chips

Bryanna's Chocolate Double-Nut Clusters

Gluten Free
Soy Free

Makes 18 to 24 candies

1 cup semi-sweet organic dairy-
  free chocolate chips
1 tablespoon maple syrup or agave
  nectar
1 tablespoon coconut oil
1/2 cup nut butter of your choice
  (page 7)
1 cup chopped toasted nuts of
  choice

This recipe is from Bryanna Clark Grogan, author of numerous vegan cookbooks including World Vegan Feast. *Bryanna always make these easy and delicious nut clusters for Christmas and Easter.*

Combine and melt the chocolate chips, maple syrup, coconut oil, and nut butter in the top of a double boiler over simmering water. When the mixture has melted and is smooth, stir in the nuts.

Drop by spoonfuls on baking parchment-lined baking sheets. Refrigerate until firm. Store in a covered container in the refrigerator

Chocolate Macadamia Truffles with Coconut

When you love chocolate, macadamia nuts, and coconut, there's only one thing to do – make these decadently delicious truffles.

Finely chop the coconut by pulsing it in a food processor. Set aside.

Place the chocolate in a heatproof bowl and set it over a small saucepan of simmering water until the chocolate melts. (Alternatively, melt the chocolate chips by placing them in a small microwaveable bowl and microwave on high for about 1 1/2 minutes, or just until the chocolate is completely melted.) Add the macadamia butter and coconut milk and blend until smooth and creamy.

Place the chocolate mixture, sugar, and 1/3 cup of the reserved coconut into a food processor and process until well combined.

Shape the mixture into 1-inch balls and roll them in the remaining 1 cup coconut, pressing so the coconut adheres to the truffles. Place the truffles on a platter or a baking sheet. Cover and refrigerate until ready to use.

Gluten Free
Soy Free

Makes 12

1 1/3 cups shredded unsweetened coconut
1/3 cup semisweet vegan chocolate chips
1/3 cup macadamia butter (page 7)
3 tablespoons coconut milk
2/3 cup confectioners' sugar

MACADAMIAS

Buttery macadamias makes a rich nut butter that is delicious in desserts and sauces. It has a slight natural sweetness and tends to be thinner than other nut butters.

Power Ball Energy Bites

Gluten Free
Soy Free

Makes 12

3/4 cup old-fashioned oats

1/2 cup toasted walnuts

2 tablespoons vegan protein powder (I use Sun Warrior vanilla)

2 tbsp cocoa powder

1 teaspoon cinnamon

1 ripe banana, cut into chunks

2 tablespoons almond butter (page 7)

1/4 cup maple syrup

1/2 cup dried cranberries

2 tablespoons ground flaxseeds

1 cup shredded toasted coconut, ground

Ideal for on-the-go breakfasts or between meal snacks, these tasty little no-bake bites pack a nutritious punch of protein, potassium, and other nutrients. If you don't have protein powder for this recipe, you can just leave it out. If the texture is too moist, add a bit more oats or walnuts to the mixture. Gluten note: Be sure your oats are labeled "certified gluten-free."

In a food processor, combine oats, walnuts, protein powder, cocoa powder, and cinnamon. Pulse until well mixed. Add the banana, almond butter, and maple syrup. Pulse until combined. Add the cranberries and flaxseeds, and pulse until combined.

Shape the mixture into 1-inch balls. If the balls are too soft, refrigerate or freeze them for an hour. Roll the balls in the ground coconut.

Transfer to a platter and refrigerate until firm, about 1 hour. Store tightly covered in the refrigerator.

Peanut Butter Flitch

This old-fashioned pinwheel candy known as flitch was a favorite in the coal region of northeastern Pennsylvania where I grew up. Cook the potato in the microwave or the oven; boiling will make it too watery. You will need about 1/2 cup of mashed potato. The amount of confectioners' sugar needed will depend on the amount of moisture in the potato. The drier the potato, the less sugar you will need to form the dough. To be safe, I usually keep a backup box of sugar in the pantry.

Place the mashed potato in a bowl. Mix in the sugar a little at a time, until the mixture reaches a dough-like consistency.

Arrange a piece of plastic wrap on a flat work surface and sprinkle a small amount of confectioners' sugar on it. Place the dough on the sugar, and top with a little more sugar and another piece of plastic wrap. Roll the mixture out to just under 1/4-inch thickness. Remove the top layer of plastic and discard.

Spread the peanut butter on top of the dough, then roll up tightly (using the plastic wrap as a guide) into a round cylinder. Cover and refrigerate until chilled, about 30 minutes. (The cylinder may flatten out a bit while it cools, so you may need to reshape it slightly about halfway through the chilling process.) Cut the roll crosswise into 1/4-inch-thick slices and arrange on a plate to serve.

Gluten Free
Soy Free

Makes 32

1 small potato, cooked, peeled, and mashed to equal 1/2 cup
1 (16-ounce) box confectioners' sugar, or more
3/4 cup peanut butter, at room temperature (page 7)

Too-Easy Chocolate-Peanut Butter Fudge

Gluten Free
Soy-Free Option

Makes 36 pieces

8 ounces semisweet vegan chocolate, coarsely chopped, or vegan chocolate chips
1 cup peanut butter (page 7)
1/2 cup vegan butter
1 cup confectioners' sugar
1 teaspoon vanilla extract

This fudge is too easy not to make on a regular basis! It firms up quickly, so be sure to get it into the pan right away. For a soy-free fudge, use a soy-free vegan butter.

Lightly grease an 8-inch square baking pan.

Place the chocolate, peanut butter, and butter in a heat-proof bowl and set it over a saucepan of simmering water, stirring until the chocolate melts and the mixture is smooth.

Turn off the heat. Whisk in the sugar and vanilla until smooth and well blended.

Scrape the mixture into the prepared pan and cool until firm. Cut into 1 1/2-inch squares. Keep refrigerated.

DOGS LOVE PEANUT BUTTER, TOO!

If you want to make something special for your best friend, try this yummy doggie treat recipe. It's made with such delicious ingredients that your four-legger may not be the only one begging for these treats.

Peanut Butter Doggie Treats

Makes about 12

2 cups whole-wheat flour
3/4 cup peanut butter (page 7)
1 ripe banana, peeled and mashed
1/4 cup wheat germ
1/2 cup nondairy milk
1/4 cup neutral vegetable oil

Preheat the oven to 350°F. Lightly grease a baking sheet. In a bowl, combine all of the ingredients and mix together until evenly combined but not sticky. Knead until smooth.

Roll out the dough and cut into shapes with your favorite cookie cutters. Arrange on the prepared baking sheet. Bake until lightly browned, 12 to 15 minutes, or a little longer if your pup prefers a crunchy cookie. Cool completely.

Acknowledgments

There are many wonderful people who had a hand in helping to make this book what it is.

First, I'd like to thank Julieanna Hever for writing the enlightening Foreword to this book. Her tireless commitment to sharing her knowledge of vegan nutrition is a force for good in this world.

Thanks also to my talented colleagues who shared their wonderful recipes in this book: Nava Atlas, Bryanna Clark Grogan, Allison Rivers Samson, and Lea Jacobson – their cooking skills are only exceeded by their generosity of spirit.

I am also most grateful to my fabulous recipe testers: Jonathan and Nancy Shanes, Lea Jacobson, Lori Maffei, Lyndsay Orwig, Vegan Aide, and Barbara Bryan. Their enthusiasm and helpful feedback made working on this book an absolute pleasure.

An extra-special acknowledgement goes to photographer Lori Maffei who, in addition to testing several of the recipes, also took the gorgeous photographs found inside the book and on its cover. A big thanks to Lori for being such a joy to work with and for making my recipes come to life with her gorgeous photographs.

Most of all, I want to thank my husband Jon Robertson, not just for his ongoing help and support for my work, but also for taking on this project as a publisher. Much gratitude to Jon, and everyone at Vegan Heritage Press, especially editor Jenna Patton, who helped make this book a reality.

I also want to thank my longtime agent Stacey Glick who many years ago suggested that I write a peanut butter cookbook. If I hadn't written that book back then, this book you have in your hands may not have existed.

About the Author

Robin Robertson is a vegan chef and award-winning cookbook author whose culinary experience spans nearly thirty years. She has been a chef, caterer, cooking teacher, and food columnist. Her bestselling cookbooks include *Vegan Planet, Quick-Fix Vegan, Fresh from the Vegan Slow Cooker, Vegan on the Cheap, 1,000 Vegan Recipes,* and *Vegan Fire & Spice.*

Robin's features and columns regularly appear in *VegNews Magazine* and online. Her articles have also appeared in *Vegetarian Times, Cooking Light, Natural Health, Better Nutrition, Health, Restaurant Business,* and other magazines.

Robin works from her home, an 1833 farmhouse in the Shenandoah Valley of Virginia that she shares with her husband, Jon, four cats, and more ducks than she can count.

Follow Robin on Facebook and Twitter (@globalvegan) as well as on her website: www.robinrobertson.com.

Appendix
Equivalents Charts and Nutritional Data

U.S. Dry Volume Measurements	
Measure	**Equivalent**
1/16 teaspoon	a dash
1/8 teaspoon	a pinch
3 teaspoons	1 tablespoon
1/8 cup	2 tablespoons
1/4 cup	4 tablespoons
1/3 cup	5 tblsp + 1 tsp
1/2 cup	8 tablespoons
3/4 cup	12 tablespoons
1 cup	16 tablespoons
1 pound	16 ounces

U.S. Liquid Volume Measurements	
8 fluid ounces	1 cup
1 pint	2 cups (16 fluid oz.)
1 quart	2 pints (4 cups)
1 gallon	4 quarts (16 cups)

U.S. to Metric Conversions	
U.S.	**Metric**
1 teaspoon	5 ml
1 tablespoon	15 ml
1 fluid ounce	30ml
1 cup	240 ml
2 cups (1 pint)	470 ml
4 cups (1 quart)	.95 liter
4 quarts (1 gallon)	3.8 liters
1 ounce	28 grams
1 pound	454 grams

Oven Temperature Conversions		
Fahrenheit	**Celsius**	**Gas Mark**
275°F	140°C	Gas mark 1 (cool)
275°F	150°C	Gas mark 2
325°F	165°C	Gas mark 3 (very moderate)
350°F	190°C	Gas mark 4 (moderate)
375°F	200°C	Gas mark 5
400°F	210°C	Gas mark 6 (moderately hot)
425°F	220°C	Gas mark 7 (hot)
450°F	230°C	Gas mark 9
475°F	240°C	Gas mark 10 (very hot)

Chart 1: Energy, Fat, Phytosterols, and Fiber in a 1-oz. Serving of Selected Nuts

Nut (1 ounce)	Energy (kcal)	Total Fat (g)	MUFA * (g)	PUFA * (g)	Phytoster-ols (mg)	Fiber (g)
Almonds	163	14.0	8.8	3.4	39	3.5
Brazil Nuts	186	18.8	7.0	5.8	N/A	2.1
Cashews	163	13.1	7.7	2.2	45	0.9
Hazelnuts	178	17.2	12.9	2.2	27	2.7
Macadamias	204	21.5	16.7	0.4	33	2.4
Peanuts (legume)	161	14.0	6.9	4.4	62	2.4
Pecans	196	20.4	11.6	6.1	29	2.7
Pistachio nuts	158	12.6	6.6	3.8	61	2.9
Walnuts, Black	175	16.7	4.3	9.9	31	1.9

*MUFA, Monounsaturated Fatty Acids; PUFA, Polyunsaturated Fatty Acids. Chart from:
http://lpi.oregonstate.edu/infocenter/foods/nuts/

Chart 2: Protein, Calcium, and Other Nutrients in a 1-oz. Serving of Selected Nuts

Nut per 1 oz. (28 grams)	Pro-tein (g)	Cal-cium (mg)	Potas-sium (mg)	Iron (mg)	Zinc (mg)	Niacin (mg)	Vitamin B$_6$ (Puridoxine) (mg)
Almonds	6	76	202	1.1	0.94	1.0	0.04
Brazil Nuts	7	45	187	0.7	1.15	0.08	0.03
Cashews	4.3	11	187	1.7	1.59	0.4	0.07
Chestnuts	0.57	13	203	0.5	0.07	0.2	0.07
Hazelnuts	4.3	35	214	1.2	0.71	0.6	0.18
Macadamias	2.2	20	103	0.7	0.37	0.6	0.1
Peanuts	7.3	26	200	1.3	0.93	3.4	1.0
Pecans	2.7	20	120	0.8	1.44	0.3	0.05
Pistachios	5.9	30	285	1.1	0.66	0.4	0.3
Walnuts, Black	4.3	28	125	0.8	0.88	0.3	0.2
Sesame Seeds	4.8	37	115	2.1	2.90	1.5	0.04
Sunflower Seeds	5.5	20	241	1.1	1.50	2.0	0.2

(Source: USDA National Nutrient Database for Standard Reference. http://ndb.nal.usda.gov/)

Gluten-Free Recipes

The following lists provide quick reference for gluten-free recipes and those offering gluten-free options.

Recipes with Gluten-Free Options

9. Desserts

Soy-Free Recipes

The following lists provide quick reference for gluten-free recipes and those offering gluten-free options.

2. Soups

3. Starters

4. Salads

5. Side Dishes

6. Main Dishes

7. Sandwiches

Recipes with Soy-Free Options

Index

Also from Vegan Heritage Press

Vegan Heritage Press is an independent book publishing company dedicated to publishing products that promote healthful living and respect for all life. Our goal is to bring to the marketplace innovative vegan cooking ideas that will delight longtime vegans, inspire newcomers, and intrigue the curious who want to improve their health and the world around them by preparing excellent plant-based recipes.

Practically Raw
Flexible Raw Recipes Anyone Can Make

AMBER SHEA CRAWLEY

This truly innovative raw food recipe book offers cooked options on many of the recipes. Also new is that all 140 dishes can be made with or without specialized equipment or ingredients. With creative, satisfying recipes, clever tips, and full-color photos, the book will appeal to seasoned raw foodists, newbies, and anyone who wants flexible, high-nutrition food. Paperback, 256 pages, ISBN: 978-0-9800131-5-3, full-color throughout, $19.95.

Vegan Fire & Spice
200 Sultry and Savory Global Recipes

ROBIN ROBERTSON

Take a trip around the world with delicious, mouthwatering recipes ranging from mildly spiced to nearly incendiary. Explore the spicy cuisines of the U.S., South America, Mexico, the Caribbean, Europe, Africa, the Middle East, India, and Asia with Red-Hot White Bean Chili, Jambalaya, Szechuan Noodle Salad, Vindaloo Vegetables, and more. Organized by global region, this book gives you 200 inventive and delicious recipes for easy-to-make international dishes, using readily available ingredients. You can adjust the heat yourself and enjoy these recipes hot – or not. Paperback, 268 pages, ISBN: 978-0-9800131-0-8, $18.95.

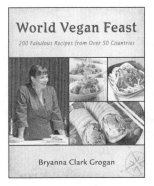

World Vegan Feast
175 Homestyle Recipes from 38 Countries

BRYANNA CLARK GROGAN

Leading vegan cooking expert Bryanna Clark Grogan shares recipes from her 22 years of experience in international cuisines. The book includes authentic dishes from around the world, an international bread sampler, gluten-free and soy-free options, as well as helpful sidebars, tips, and menus. This book features recipes you won't find in other vegan cookbooks. Paperback, 272 pages, ISBN: 978-0-9800131-4-6, 36 color photos, $19.95

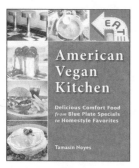

American Vegan Kitchen
Delicious Comfort Food from Blue Plate Specials to Homestyle Favorites

TAMASIN NOYES

Use these recipes to make your own vegan versions of favorite comfort food dishes found in diners, delis, and cafes across America. They satisfy vegans and non-vegans alike with deli sandwiches, scrumptious burgers and fries, pastas, pizzas, omelets, pancakes, casseroles, and desserts. Paperback, 232 pages, ISBN: 978-0-9800131-1-5, $18.95.

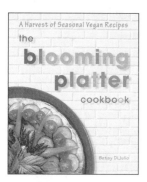

Vegan Unplugged
A Pantry Cuisine Cookbook and Survival Guide

JON ROBERTSON WITH RECIPES BY ROBIN ROBERTSON

Vegan Unplugged is your go-to source for gourmet pantry cooking. These easy recipes can be made in fifteen minutes or less. The book is ideal for camping, boating, or anytime you just don't feel like cooking. It's also a "must have" during power outages with great-tasting, nutritionally balanced pantry cuisine. Paperback, 216 pages, ISBN: 978-0-9800131-2-2, $14.95.

The Blooming Platter Cookbook
A Harvest of Seasonal Vegan Recipes

BETSY DIJULIO

A celebration of fresh, seasonal produce, this book features a wide range of recipes from easy homestyle dishes to creative upscale fare including American favorites and global cuisines. The 175 recipes showcase the taste, beauty, and nutrition of seasonal ingredients. Also includes recipe variations, menu suggestions, seasonal icons, and tips. Paperback, 224 pages, 36 color photos, ISBN: 978-0-9800131-3-9, $18.95.

Spring 2013

Practically Raw Desserts
Flexible Recipes for All-Natural Sweets and Treats

AMBER SHEA CRAWLEY

This treasure of raw cakes, cookies, brownies, pies, puddings, candies, pastries, and frozen treats, can be made 100% raw or adapted to a non-raw kitchen, with many cooked options. The desserts are free of animal products, gluten, wheat, soy, corn, refined grains, refined sugars, yeast, starch, and other nutrient-poor ingredients. Contains nutritional data, a pantry guide, variations, substitutions, and icons. Paperback, 242 pages, ISBN: 978-0-9800131-8-4, All Color, $19.95.